WAYNE OTTO
DAVID FORD

University of
Wisconsin

TEACHING
ADULTS TO READ

HOUGHTON MIFFLIN COMPANY · BOSTON
New York · Atlanta · Geneva, ILL. · Dallas · Palo Alto

The materials review in Chapter 4 was undertaken and published as a project of the Research and Development Center for Learning and Re-Education at the University of Wisconsin, Madison, Wisconsin. Its preparation was supported by a contract with the United States Office of Education, Department of Health, Education, and Welfare, under the provisions of the Cooperative Research Program.

"In all ages men have fought
most desperately for beautiful
cities yet to be built and gardens
yet to be planted."

Eric Hoffer
The True Believer

FOREWORD

Teaching adults to read has become a necessity rather than a luxury. In our mechanized and affluent society we have the paradox of shortages of educated and technically trained manpower on the one hand and heavy unemployment among illiterates on the other hand. Our modern culture has six million functionally illiterate adults. This fact has created a major national crisis that can no longer be tolerated.

The problem was first felt during World War II, when rapid mobilization of the army brought to light thousands of young men who were functionally illiterate and could not learn to become effective military personnel. The military services found it necessary to establish special training units to teach these functionally illiterate soldiers to read and write. In the midst of a war, the army had to set up schools.

A similar situation exists today. Our social imbalances have caused unemployment among the uneducated, school dropouts, public assistance, racial unrest, and abnormal utilization of manpower. To make matters worse, a higher level of intelligence and literacy than ever before is demanded by the complexity of modern living and a country that believes in a "government of the people, by the people, and for the people." These are some of the reasons why local, state, and federal units of government have developed programs of basic education for the millions of adults over 25. Instructors of adults in these basic training programs such as the Job Corps, the Manpower Development Program, and other adult education programs are eagerly seeking methods and materials that can be used effectively in literacy training programs.

Teaching adults to read and write cannot be accomplished

with a one-system approach. Adults, perhaps even more than children, differ in their levels of attainment, in their methods of learning, and in the materials to which they respond best. It is the responsibility of the instructor (1) to use the best methods of teaching for a particular group, and (2) to select the most appropriate materials for a particular individual or group of individuals.

Teaching Adults to Read is not a one-method approach or a detailed step-by-step text book on how to teach a class of functionally illiterate adults. It is a guide book from which instructors may select a variety of materials, methods, and ideas. It contains: (a) a description of some of the problems of adult illiterates, (b) basic principles of instruction in reading, and (c) a well organized and detailed outline of selected materials from which the instructor can select appropriate materials for his trainees. *Teaching Adults to Read* serves as a basic reference for methods and materials that instructors of the functionally illiterate can ill afford to be without.

Samuel A. Kirk

PREFACE

Some time ago William S. Gray wrote about helping children to be "on their own" in reading. He was concerned with bringing children to the point in their reading skill development where, having mastered the mechanics, they could function with relative independence. The primary focus of this book is upon helping adults to be on their own in reading. The scope is from illiteracy to approximately fourth-grade-level ability. The goal is to help illiterate and marginally literate adults to reach a level of reading skill that will permit them to cope with the reading tasks that confront them in their daily lives. Assuredly the development and growth of reading skills is a lifetime process; our concern is with laying the foundation of basic skills that permits future development.

Our hope is that this book will serve as a handbook for literacy instructors. If there are few pat answers, it is because there are few pat questions; the content of adult basic reading classes must vary as greatly as the needs of the adults who enroll in them. The instructor who has reasonable freedom from rigid administrative control and at least average versatility should find information and suggestions that will be useful.

We have included background material not because we think that literacy instructors are likely to be ignorant of the nature and scope of the illiteracy problem but because we feel that to re-examine the general problems of illiterates and the marginally literate is worthwhile as an overview and as a means for establishing a framework for considering the instructional program in basic reading. A point in particular that seems to merit belaboring is that many of the marginally literate are not adults who have never been taught; instead they are adults who have — for a vast array of compelling reasons — failed to learn to read. To approach these people as if they were beginning first-graders would be as wrong as to approach them as slow learners or retardates. The *problem* of illiteracy is a national concern; but the *problems* of illiteracy are of personal concern to the illiterate. Literacy instructors need to go all the way in developing genuine empathy.

We have also included lists and evaluations of representa-tive teaching materials, appropriate reading materials for the newly literate, and tests. The extensive evaluations of pub-lishers' programs for teaching the basic reading skills should be particularly useful. The approaches covered vary widely, so the reviews given should help instructors with the task of choosing appropriate materials for particular groups. The amount of formal testing in an adult basic reading program will be limited, but familiarity with the tests discussed will help instructors to personalize their teaching in terms of indi-vidual and group needs. In general, we have attempted to present a variety rather than a package of materials and a paradigm rather than a prescription for a program of adult basic reading instruction.

Finally, we have discussed the problems of scope and se-quence in a program of basic reading skill development as well as techniques and procedures for implementing the pro-gram. Again, the intent was to familiarize and review more than to prescribe. The specifics of a program must necessarily be worked out in view of the demands of the situation. Our hope is that this book will truly serve as a handbook for work-ing out the specifics.

Wayne Otto
David Ford

CONTENTS

TEACHING ADULTS TO READ

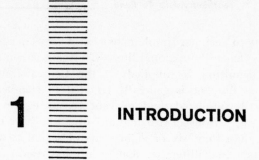

1   INTRODUCTION

Recently our affluent, highly literate nation has begun to recognize more openly and to attack more vigorously the problem of adult illiteracy. The problem, of course, is not a new one, but the magnitude of the attack is new. Resources have been made available that make it feasible to execute needed educational programs.

This rapid move to massive action in an area where there have been disinterest and inertia has brought a number of associated problems into focus. There is, for example, a drastic shortage of personnel trained to do a creditable job of teaching adults to read. More basic, there are unanswered questions regarding the methods and materials for teaching adults to read. Yet there is no excuse for inaction. Much is known about adult learning, many materials do exist, and teachers have always come forward to meet new challenges. Our purpose, then, is to help new teachers of basic reading for adults to make use of existing information and materials.

• ILLITERACY DEFINED

The Census Bureau defines an illiterate as a person 10 years old or over who responds negatively to the question, "Can you read and write?" The implication is that the person cannot both read and write a simple message either in English or in any other language. So restricted a definition is of limited usefulness, for the reading demands of a complex society go far

1

beyond ability to decipher simple messages. A more meaningful concept is that of "functional literacy." Again, a common operational definition is supplied by the Census Bureau. Educational attainment is generally equated to number of years of school completed, and relevant census figures are available. Thus, persons 25 years old and over who have completed fewer than four, six or eight years of school may be designated functional illiterates. Some confusion results from lack of general agreement about what number of years should be the criterion, but once a number has been selected, this definition has the advantage of being straightforward. In practice, many writers do cite the census figures regarding years of schooling in discussing the magnitude of the limited literacy problem.

Unfortunately, though, this definition is as arbitrary as it is straightforward. Completion of a given number of years' schooling does not assure skill development or educational attainment at that level. Secondary teachers can attest to the fact that high schools are graduating some pupils who cannot read at even a fourth grade level. Whether the cause is limited intelligence, extreme learning problems, poor teaching, cultural deprivation or any of a host of other factors is beside the point. The fact is that years' exposure to school may be only grossly related to achievement, and the problem is likely to be greater than the census figures indicate. Of course, one might optimistically point out that some adults who read very well learned to do so with little formal schooling. In any event, it seems clear that years of schooling, while a convenient criterion, is only a gross indicator of functional literacy.

In an article for *Adult Leadership,* Esther Fox (*1964*) attempted to define functional illiteracy by example:

> The illiterate adult in American society is that individual who does not have the necessary reading skills to make him eligible for vocational training when his marginal job in the labor market is discontinued. His lack of reading skills serves to make him and to keep him unemployable. His functional reading may be on a

number of levels, varying from preprimer to that of the word-by-word reader who does not comprehend what he reads. He may well be of that 25 per cent of the population which is trainable but below average in intelligence. . . . Or he may be of average intelligence but of that unfortunate group of individuals who have been educationally deprived.

The disadvantage of this definition is that it makes the task of categorizing adults as functional illiterates a matter of individual diagnosis, so that the task of estimating the magnitude of the problem becomes extremely complex. Nevertheless, it seems desirable to define functional illiteracy in terms of lack of ability to function in everyday situations.

Functional illiteracy, then, is perhaps most realistically defined in terms of the needs of both individuals and the society of which they are a part. Whereas the ability to decipher simple messages may have been adequate as a functional skill in the past, this is no longer so in most situations. Individuals who cannot read fluently are not only likely to be unable to function effectively on the job; they are quite likely to be unable even to apply for new jobs. But certainly all jobs do not require the same level of reading skill: functional skill in one area may be far from functional in another. Clearly, there is need for a sliding scale in defining functional literacy.

In the present context, the functionally literate adult is one who is able to read and write with relative independence. That is, he has mastered the essential word recognition skills in reading and the letter forms in writing, and is able to use these skills as tools for obtaining information and expressing his own thoughts. This basic level of skill development is roughly equivalent to that typically attained by children in the first four years of school.

• THE ILLITERACY PROBLEM

Although there are complications in defining illiteracy, some estimate of the scope of the problem in the United States today is needed. As already stated, Census Bureau figures provide a straightforward means for estimating the magnitude of the illiteracy — or marginal literacy — problem. The figures in Table 1, from the 1960 census, are, for example, often cited in the literature dealing with problems in adult basic education.

**TABLE 1: Years of Schooling Completed
by Adults Age 25 and Older (in thousands)**

Group	Adults Age 25 and Older	Years of Education		
		None	1–4	5–6
Total population	99,438	2,274 (2.3%)	6,027 (6.1%)	7,422 (7.5%)
White	89,581	1,720 (1.9%)	4,268 (4.8%)	5,987 (6.7%)
Non-White	9,856	554 (5.6%)	1,759 (17.8%)	1,435 (14.6%)

SOURCE: U.S. Department of Commerce, Bureau of the Census, *U.S. Census of Population: 1960, General, Social and Economic Characteristics,* PC series.

These data make it clear that many adults are undereducated. Reasons why the data may not provide an appropriate basis for accurate estimates of the number of functional illiterates have been pointed out, but the figures probably do represent minimum numbers at each level.

Undoubtedly many older persons are included in each of the categories of low educational attainment. Nevertheless, the problem is likely to continue for many years. The Census Bureau estimates that, if present trends continue, by 1980 there will be still more than five million persons age 25 or older with fewer than five years of schooling and 21.5 million with fewer than eight years. Some details of the projected educational attainment are included in Table 2.

The figures given in Table 1 include institutionalized persons, many of whom obviously are not candidates for basic education programs. Also undoubtedly included are many slow learners — persons with IQ's in the 80 to 90 range, whose capacities are limited but who are capable of at least eighth grade attainment — who chose to terminate their education early rather than attempt to cope with instructional programs not adapted to their unique needs. Not included are persons who for many reasons (*Otto and McMenemy, 1966*) never mastered even the most basic academic skills but remained in school, probably because of compulsory attendance laws or

TABLE 2: Projected Educational Attainment

Years of School Completed	Millions of Persons 25 Years and Over			
	1950	1960	1970	1980
13+	11.9	15.7	20.4	28.2
9–12	33.3	44.8	57.3	76.0
5–8	32.6	30.5	26.0	21.5
0–4	9.8	8.0	6.4	5.2
Total	87.5	99.0	110.0	130.8

SOURCE: U.S. Department of Health, Education and Welfare based on data appearing in *Current Population Reports, Population Characteristics*, Series P-20, No. 91 published by the U.S. Department of Commerce, Bureau of the Census.

other pressures, for eight or more years. Both of the latter groups comprise adults who are functional illiterates, and both groups need special treatment because they have failed to learn despite the fact that they have been exposed to teaching. A point that should be clear is that not only those who have not attended school are illiterate; many functional illiterates have attended school, some of them for eight years or more. Such people should not be excluded from basic education programs, but neither should they be treated as if they had never been to school. Special effort is needed to help them to overcome the negative perceptions they are likely to have acquired.

The troublesome fact is that many adults who have had — or at least claim to have had — six or more years of schooling have not mastered basic reading and writing skills. A case in point is a study (*Hilliard, 1963*) in the Woodlawn area of Chicago. Of the population sample, 6.6 percent reported that they had not gone as far as the sixth grade in school. But when the same people were given achievement tests to determine their actual level of functioning, 50.7 percent scored below the sixth-grade level. The problem is iceberg-like: its exact proportions can be determined only by looking beneath the surface.

• PROGRESS IN REACHING THE UNDEREDUCATED

Efforts to combat undereducation have received great impetus from the federal programs included in the war on poverty. In general it seems clear that programs designed to eliminate poverty must reflect a sensitivity for the needs of the undereducated and include plans for dealing with the problem of too limited education. Minimal education and poverty are so intertwined that the two problems must be dealt with concurrently. There is, however, also specific provision for support of adult basic education programs.

Title IIb of the Economic Opportunity Act of 1964 made provision for adult basic education. This is the first federal effort to help schools teach adults to read, speak properly, write, and do arithmetic well enough to qualify for jobs or job training. Persons over the age of 18 who have completed fewer than six grades of school are given an opportunity to attend adult basic education classes. Courses are given at three levels: first through third grades; fourth through sixth grades; and seventh and eighth grades. The Office of Economic Opportunity delegates authority and allocates funds to the Department of Health, Education and Welfare to administer the program, which is conducted by the Adult Education Branch of the Office of Education. All 50 states, the District of Columbia, and three territories are now participating, and each contributes a minimum of 10 percent to the cost of its state and local programs. By the end of fiscal year 1966, $38 million in federal funds had been allocated and 373,338 persons had participated in adult basic education programs.

In addition to the specific objective of encouraging the operation of state plans for developing basic skills among hard-core undereducated adults living in poverty, Adult Basic Education has several related goals (*Office of Economic Opportunity, 1965*). One is to establish teacher-training institutes that will provide a "master teacher" in each local program who can update and guide colleagues regarding adult basic education developments. A number of these institutes have been held throughout the nation. The direct and indirect long-range effects of such efforts to develop a corps of highly competent, knowledgeable specialists are likely to be far-reaching. A second goal is to stimulate more institutions of higher education, public and private agencies, organizations, and firms to undertake programs of training for administrators of Adult Basic Education programs and others involved in the project. Development of trained leadership is basic to the continued success of the program. Other goals are to stimulate the development of research proposals that will assist in answering the complex problems being faced by program people at the local level, and to provide a clearing house of data on participants in Adult Basic Education programs for use at national, state, and local levels. The teachers and administrators trained, the information gathered and systematized, and the people salvaged will remain with us regardless of the direction taken by future federal legislation.

The federal programs have contributed much toward bringing a great national problem into clearer focus than ever before. But persons charged with the responsibility of creating and carrying out local programs ought to be aware of all of the resources available. The success of state and local programs still depends upon action at the state and local level. And we should not lose sight of the fact that vigorous local programs have been offered — under the auspices of vocational and adult schools, religious organizations, and philanthropic foundations — for years, since long before the crusade to eradicate illiteracy and marginal literacy became a national one.

• PURPOSE AND PLAN OF THE BOOK

In order to say what this book is, it seems necessary first to say what it is not. It is not a step-by-step general plan for teaching adults to read. As we have already noted, the causes for adult illiteracy are diverse. Programs for teaching basic reading must reflect the diversity if they are to succeed. To treat the unschooled, the slow learners, and the school failures the same is naive; to suggest a single plan for teaching reading to all adult functional illiterates would be delusive.

Teaching Adults to Read is an introduction to the field and a handbook for literacy instructors. Although there are no pat answers, there is an attempt to present the basic elements from which sound, sensible instructional programs can be created. The first three chapters deal with the nature of the problem of illiteracy and marginal literacy, the problems that arise when adults return to school, and characteristics of adult learners. Selected materials for teaching adults to read are presented in Chapter 4. Materials included are limited to those useful at the most basic level, the level of skill development that serves as a base for subsequent independent reading. The focus in Chapter 4 is upon relatively self-contained systems for teaching the basic reading skills, but selected supplementary materials are also discussed. Chapter 5 is a discussion of techniques and procedures for implementing a program of basic reading instruction for adults. The assumption throughout the book is that programs will be devised, and that instructors will be permitted to teach, in response to the unique needs of the students involved. Where programs are created by fiat and where the quest is for a prepackaged program, this book will not be very useful.

• **REFERENCES**

FOX, ESTHER. "Considerations in Constructing a Basic Reading Program for Functionally Illiterate Adults." *Adult Leadership,* 1964, 13, pp. 7–8.

HILLIARD, RAYMOND M. "Massive Attack on Illiteracy." *American Library Association Bulletin,* 1963, 57, pp. 1034–1039.

OTTO, WAYNE, AND RICHARD A. MCMENEMY. *Corrective and Remedial Teaching.* Boston: Houghton Mifflin Company, 1966.

OFFICE OF ECONOMIC OPPORTUNITY. *A Nation Aroused, First Annual Report,* 1965.

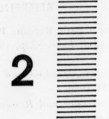

2

WHEN THE ADULT
RETURNS TO SCHOOL

In a complex, literacy-dependent, and industrial society, illiterates are a highly distinctive and enigmatic variant population. They are unlike everyone else in that education does not and has never played a significant positive role in their lives. The majority are dropouts who have quit school under socially unfortunate circumstances (*Greenleigh, 1965*). Many have left because of some pressing economic need. In urban communities now, the most common reason for illiterates' leaving school is a delinquent act. Often formally breaking school ties is clouded by an overwhelming personal problem, by a profound sense of academic failure, or by guilt feelings surrounding pregnancy. This chapter, then, is about adults who have left school under trying circumstances and who must now renew the effort to obtain a formal education.

In attempting to understand the illiterate who returns to school, it is perhaps deceptively easy to compare him with the illiterate and educationally retarded men who entered the army during World War II. By almost any standard, the educationally retarded adult soldier was outstandingly successful in learning to read. In the period subsequent to June, 1943, there were 134,981 white and 119,291 Negro graduates of army special training schools for illiterates and the educationally retarded. This represents 85.1 percent of the total program entrants!

Why were illiterates overwhelmingly successful in completing the army literacy program? According to Goldberg (*1951*), this program had several distinct motivational advantages: (1) Men felt the need to learn to read and write in order to maintain contact with family and friends and to be retained in the army as "regular" soldiers. (2) Men in the army had a well planned and well regulated day. Their housing, clothing, food, medicine, and recreational needs were provided for and they were able to provide financial support for their families. They were free to give full attention to the challenges of a socially rewarded occupation. (3) The army had unlimited funds with which to carry on a comprehensive and balanced literacy training program. (4) The army was able to procure suitable instructors and supervisors from an eight-million-man reservoir, and was able financially to hire qualified civilian instructors. (5) The literacy program was a comparatively new adventure for the army. There were no traditional procedures that had to be followed, nor were instructors unprepared or unwilling to apply the materials and techniques generally developed.

The program goal was modest, clearly formulated, and attainable: to develop fourth-grade level reading competency. A combination of circumstances in addition to the above helped to make this program successful. Trainees were motivated and they were competently instructed. All were carefully selected for training. They used instructional materials especially designed for that reading program. Reading instruction was a part of other activities that occupied the entire day. Teaching groups were small.

The important social and cultural benefits and incentives

that might motivate a nonreader to learn to read in time of war and at the conclusion of a severe economic depression are simply not available today — to our good fortune. It is possible that the problems that led originally to the termination of schooling may still be present or that others equally blocking to educational progress have taken their place. To paraphrase Cornelus Land (*1963*), an authority on adult education, we are in a position where a correct understanding of present motivations and circumstances is necessary.

The kind of determination needed to overcome illiteracy may be inferred from the types of obstacles that adults must successfully overcome in returning to school. Robert F. Barnes (*1965*) compares these difficulties to a series of barriers. The problems are: (1) economic, (2) familial, (3) social, and (4) psychological in nature.

• ECONOMIC PROBLEMS

For the vast majority of adult illiterates, returning to school means curtailment of income. It may no longer be possible to purchase necessities. A not infrequently given reason for withdrawal from literacy classes is discomfort from inadequate clothing. One lady said that the first few weeks of class were quite painful because of chilblains she contracted while traveling to class in winter without a coat. She said she could not purchase a coat and still be able to pay carfare.

Economic difficulties may lead to other equally disquieting and disruptive circumstances for the student. Mothers may be forced to choose between the uncertain help of neighbors caring for their children during class hours and hiring a baby sitter, which they can ill afford. Some schools have attempted to step into the breach by allowing small children to come to school with their parents. There, according to one recent study, the children are not apt to encounter a planned and supervised program. They may be permitted to wander the halls. Since such well-meaning aid usually is without the knowledge and support of the board of education, which bears legal responsibility for all those invited to the school, it cannot be considered a satisfactory solution to the problem of child care. Night schools usually require payment of tuition fees and the purchase of one or more textbooks. These may be major expenses for a family whose income is marginally sufficient.

Transportation is usually not an economic problem in rural illiteracy programs. Classes are often held in locations convenient to sizeable groups, such as in migratory work camps or community halls. Metropolitan programs, on the other hand, may draw their student population from a considerable distance. Traveling to and from class can itself be a major financial burden requiring a daily outlay of funds.

• FAMILIAL PROBLEMS

As was mentioned above, one problem facing mothers of small children is day care. The burden is likely to fall on relatives, friends, and neighbors, for the most part. A recent study showed that 10 percent of those students who had children requiring adult supervision in the home had them cared for on a casual basis. It was pointed out that these children may face very real dangers and the possibility of neglect. Pupils whose children are uncertainly or indifferently cared for may fear that in seeking an education they are at the same time endangering the children and, concomitantly, their efficiency as students will be reduced. Some welfare agencies are reluctant to refer illiterate mothers to schools if child care funds are not available. Fortunately some A.D.C. (Aid for Dependent Children) and public welfare recipients are provided with child care funds or baby sitting services. This should facilitate both attendance and active participation in learning activities.

For the school to provide adequate care for children during class hours may be a step in the right direction. But by itself it is a poor substitute for a program that offers a variety of learning experiences for children. One plan suggested (*Green-leigh, 1965*) is a total family approach to breaking the chain of social deprivation and illiteracy:

> The most effective step is the development of day-long programs in comprehensive adult education centers. Ideally, the center would be open in the evening as well as during the day and would provide a cluster of service activities for children — organized pre-school programs, nursery school activities, kindergarten activities, adult services, free lunch programs, enrichment programs, etc. In addition, the center would provide, of course, full-time, day-long education for the parents. Centers could be open in the evenings for older children.

At least one favorable outcome can be expected from skillfully involving the entire family in a program centered around their needs and interests. It has been suggested that the army reading program was successful because reading training was merged with other day-long activities. Besides increasing motivation, which should attract new enrollees, prevent dropouts, and regularize attendance, the family's image of the school as an institution should be changed so that education is seen as a useable tool to obtain economic security.

Minor children can be a mother's greatest source of strength. They may also be one of the most powerful barriers to her returning to school. They may see the parent's enrollment as depriving them of support and attention during critical hours of the day. And for this reason they may pressure her by a variety of ingenious maneuvers not to attend class. Older family members who are not so dependent may also disapprove of the pupil's educational endeavors. They may show overt hostility by refusing the cooperation in household chores that would free her from housework. Or they may cooperate reluctantly. Often these feelings are disguised as kidding: they might tell the pupil that returning to school is a childish activity. Many parents report, however, that their children are the most supportive family members in their adjustment to school (*Greenleigh, 1965*).

Some familial barriers are within the household environment. Living arrangements can interfere with educational processes. Many adult students live in overcrowded living units. It is often difficult under crowded conditions to establish one place to prepare lessons. In one study, 70 percent of the adult students had from one to six people living with them. Typically, there was less than one room per family member. Students also need and may not have: sufficient light in their study place, a suitable chair and table, and sufficient ventilation. In one study, a third of all pupils rated these conditions as fair to poor in their study areas.

Finally, the home environment may fail to encourage the adult illiterate. There may, for example, be few reading materials in the home that would support reading skills once developed. As shown in Table 1, a little over one third of the

TABLE 1: Reading Materials in 885 Homes of Illiterates

Reading Materials	Number[a]	Percent
Newspapers	535	60.4
Magazines	340	38.4
Books	348	39.3

[a] Total is greater than the sample because some students had more than one item.

SOURCE: Used with permission of Greenleigh Associates, Inc., 1965.

homes of 885 illiterates surveyed had either books or magazines, while over 60 percent contained newspapers. Some of these homes doubtless had more than one item of reading material but many more did not. Some literacy instructors have found it desirable to give away pamphlets and paperback books as an out-of-class supplement to learning activities, a practice justified by the information in the accompanying table.

Family money habits may also create problems. Unsound installment purchasing and small loans obtained by many lower-class families, which are partly the result of established habits and partly the result of economic necessity, can lead to the removal of critical items of furniture, such as beds and appliances, by agents of lending companies in the satisfaction of debts. The family check may be delayed or withheld. Often families are living so close to the economic margin that at times the student may not be able to afford public transportation to class.

• SOCIAL PROBLEMS

The third barrier to overcoming illiteracy is *social*. Social pressures determine whether or not the pupil will enroll and whether he will or will not remain in the program. (This is discussed in Chapter 3.) Many illiterates have carefully built social habits that help them to avoid situations where reading or writing might be required. Their fear is a reflection of the generally held belief that illiteracy is a sign of stupidity.

The influence of social groups upon the illiterate enrollee can be observed directly. In rural areas of the Southeast, it is customary for learning activities of adults and learning activities of young people to differ in both organization and content. In an interview noted by Barnes (*1965*) one student said: "The toughest part about startin' in this class was listenin' to my friends telling me that 'you're too old to learn anything in books, and besides school is for kids.' Now that I'm in school, they don't say anything — they just look at me and grin." An emerging literate may have to learn to cope with suspicion when he evidences new verbal habits. He may receive little encouragement from his peers to continue the educational process.

• PSYCHOLOGICAL PROBLEMS

Failure to become literate in a society where illiteracy plays an essential part in maintaining social contacts must be considered an extremely stressful experience with profound psychological significance. Each illiterate must learn to cope with both failure and fear of failure. The fourth barrier, then, which the pupil faces in returning to school is *psychological*. Fear of academic failure is particularly associated with

extent, his social activity. Both underachievement and over-achievement have been identified with the same physical abnormality. A recent book by Beatrice A. Wright (*1960*) presents a readable account of psychological adjustment to physical disability. For teachers of older illiterates, it is particularly important to recognize how the dynamics of learning may involve adjustment to aging.

• **Psychosomatic difficulties.** Psychosomatic behaviors are related to disturbances involving the organs of internal economy and instinctual function and to the body image as a whole (*Noyes and Kolb, 1963*). Here the disturbances themselves are the adjustment mechanism. These may involve the reading act. An aversion to school may seem to trigger asthmatic attacks, for example.

• **Maladroitness.** In instances of maladroitness reading difficulty is associated with personal disorganization and social aberration having no necessary physiological involvement.

Intra-cultural Barriers

The customs and activities of the group to which the learner belongs (and which he shares) may interfere with his learning to read. They may be linguistic practices. They may involve the *production* of language, such as constraints on how and when language is to be used. Or they may involve group practices that inhibit intellectual growth or performance.

• **Language differences.** There may be discrepancies between the language customarily used by the learner and the language as it appears in print and as it is taught. To some extent the language of each individual varies from that of every other. But where the variance is associated with group practices — where social mechanisms are involved — a particularly difficult situation arises for the learner since new learning must compete with old established language habits. Lisping, for example, may be "cute" at home, but it handicaps oral discriminations. There are at least two types of language habits that interfere with learning new ones: *dialectic differences,* where the forms of language including phonemics (sounds), morphemics (word forms), and syntactics (word arrangements) differ; and *logistic differences,* where the structure of the language used may or may not differ but where the language content does.

· **Learned behavioral patterns.** Some motor, perceptual, and verbal habits that are acceptable to a group are not tolerated in the classroom. The boy who expresses himself with his fists rather than orally and the girl who "visits" constantly may be displaying behavior patterns that are approved of by their families and "normal" for their social group and age. The tendency not to respond may also be present. Almost every teacher has been faced with the situation where she cannot persuade a student to respond with an answer he obviously knows.

· **Experiential limitations.** Some cultural group activities or beliefs limit the incentives necessary for intellectual growth or interest. The belief is widely held among rural whites of Appalachia that education alienates children from their parents. Farm families have traditionally opposed children's using plowing time to attend class. In the former instance, children may be actively discouraged from being interested in school; in the latter, competing activities that are acceptable to the family and farmers generally are interposed.

Inter-cultural Barriers

The members of one culture face socially related difficulties in learning the literate patterns of another. These difficulties include all of the problems that sub-cultural group members have learning the literate language of the society. Two areas of difficulty are identified.

· **Second-language problems.** Language habits already learned may interfere with the establishment of new ones. Differences in phonemic, morphemic and syntactical structures as well as psychological differences reflected in language usage may make learning to read more difficult.

• **Non-language differences.** Other barriers include both learned behavioral patterns that make learning difficult and limitations of experience common to a culture that does not place a premium upon intellectual interest and growth. Learning to read may mean that the reader must overcome powerful forces, which initially shaped his character. He may have to put aside old customs, old roles, and even old beliefs about himself. In some instances learning to read means that the individual must renounce the support of the culture in which he was raised.

Hereditary-Genetic Barriers

According to MacDonald Critcheley, reading disorders are organic rather than psychogenic and genetic rather than situational. Few reading authorities share this point of view. That physiological conditions affect learning processes, however, is not to be denied. Oettinger (*1963*) identifies eight genetic deficiencies that may unfavorably influence the development of reading behavior: hypomentia, inherited dysrhythmias, inherited metabolic diseases, inherited visual defects, inherited speech and hearing defects, inherited dominance defects, slow maturation, and epilepsy.

Physiological-Acquired Barriers

Oettinger (*1963*) also identifies five acquired conditions that may retard or prevent the development of reading. These are: hypomentia, traumatic brain injuries, visual defects, auditory defects, and epilepsy.

Situational Barriers

Some conditions presented by the learning environment act against the learning of reading skills. These include odors, noises, a particular time of day, improper seating of pupils, and teacher ineptness.

Curricular Barriers

Some reading materials and reading skills are not suitably used by and taught to every individual. Learning word-analysis skills may prove to be a painfully slow and unrewarding activity for beginning readers. Adult non-readers who have previously been exposed to a phonic method might be more successfully taught by the whole word approach. This has been the experience of the army program.

Children's reading material is best left to children. It is degrading and confirms all of the unfavorable opinions of self generated by initial reading failure for an adult non-reader to be presented with learning tasks from elementary school books.

Planning to Overcome Barriers

Problems associated with reading disorders are not necessarily causes of reading failure in the sense that any one difficulty is invariably associated with reading failure. Nor must every difficulty necessarily be removed for progress to occur.

Faced with the very real difficulties of her students, the teacher may wish to try a variety of helpful procedures. Where learning to read has strong emotional overtones or where the difficulty has been associated with previous academic failure, one of three general strategies might be used appropriately.

1. *Overcome the problem.* Depending on the nature of the problem it may be desirable either to postpone formal reading instruction temporarily or to make reading a part of a more general ameliorative plan. Programs in which there is close cooperation between counselors, teachers, social workers, administrators, and referral agencies should contemplate a broad attack on many problems of the illiterate.

2. *Modify instructional procedure and content to avoid the problem area.* For example, it may be desirable to group according to language background or by estimates of intelli-

gence. And it may be necessary to purchase one set of materials for foreign-born illiterates, another for young adults who have dropped out of school recently, and a third for middle-aged illiterates.

3. *Modify the goals of instruction.* Where personal limitations cannot be overcome or where the procedures cannot be changed, it may be desirable to alter the aims of the program. Without careful preparation, however, goal modification may be taken by the student as a sign that the school cannot or will not help.

The army program had limited goals for quite another reason. The intent was to train readers for a specifiable task; labeling the illiterate as unteachable was avoided by integrating the goals of reading instruction into the broader aspects of educating civilians to be competent soldiers.

• ORGANIZING FOR INSTRUCTION

What can educators do to accommodate illiterate adults to a program of basic education? This problem might be resolved by deciding what techniques will most facilitate learning to read. But, because most illiterate adults are not now attracted to basic education even when they are aware that programs exist and many others quickly lose interest in learning to read, it is appropriate to consider some of the broader implications of the question.

Presumably what we do as educators is a question of what we believe ought to be done and what we can do — what imaginative organizational strategies we can employ to implement our beliefs and what instructional tactics we can develop to carry them out. Our strategies and tactics involve (1) developing an educational philosophy, (2) implementing our beliefs through the development of a facilitating administrative structure, and (3) utilizing an appropriate repertoire of instructional methods.

Developing a Practical Philosophy

As educators, our ideas may not always be employed nor our advice heeded, so that we may not feel that it is important to consider seriously the philosophical implications of what we do. There are, however, at least two reasons why this is not a viable argument. First, the commitment to adult basic literacy programs has not been widely accepted as an important social goal. Many educators, as well as the general public, are not aware that the war on poverty extends to the literacy area or that we are obliged to be in the war at all. We may need to convince others of the importance of our work. And second, the mobilization of our efforts as individuals and as a profession depends on what we wish to accomplish and how accurately we see the task. These goals should involve extensive thought and discussion. Wars, not excluding the war on poverty, are generated by conflicting points of view both among and between the combatants.

In the course of developing policies that will facilitate sound educational practice, it is apparently inevitable that the same issues arise and, to some extent, the same questions are commonly asked. While problems generalize from one educational circumstance to another, the most effective solutions are situationally relevant. All too frequently we have neither the experience nor the wisdom to anticipate what issues will arise. The unexpected difficulties were encountered by the army training program for illiterates in World War II, the Job Corps, and Community Action Programs.

The way problems are framed may determine the way their solutions are implemented. For example, high-sounding but vague goals are not easily translated into actions. Generally speaking, the more specifically and concretely the issue is stated, the more likely it is that useful solutions can be devised.

An important group of problems involves the content of the curriculum. One issue frequently raised is whether literacy training should also contain job-skill development. How

practical should a reading program be? Unless course outlines, presumably growing out of a discussion of such substan-
tive issues, are stated in terms of behavioral outcomes and
means to these ends, even the most skillful teachers will have
difficulty coming to grips with the task, and measurement will
be both inaccurate and useless.

The content of the curriculum (and hence the wording of
curriculum problems) can often be determined partly by local
conditions, such as the job market in the immediate area.
Policies may include frequent referral to these criteria.

A related issue is the extent and nature of the school's involvement with the social habits of the pupil. Should the
school teach adult illiterates how to behave appropriately in
certain sets of circumstances? For example: Should adults be
taught to be punctual? Should they be taught to show hostility in socially acceptable ways? Answers to these questions
may involve two other important problems encountered, particularly in programs involving illiterates in their twenties —
namely, what scholastic implications should there be for violators of the law or social conventions and, more generally,
what part might an individual pupil play in his own education? Some educators are inclined to feel that pupils, as a
part of their training, should assume some organizational and
administrative responsibilities; many believe that each pupil
must be permitted to plan, with appropriate help, his own
educational experience.

Young adult illiterates such as those in Job Corps Centers
may, through attempts at re-establishing old habits or experimenting with new ones, become law violators. Can the school
ignore this type of behavior? If the answer is a conditional
no (or yes), then to what extent no (or yes)? Should the school
establish a set of regulations? Should the fact be faced that
with each regulation must go either a penalty or the power
to impose a penalty?

Another issue involves the use of a system of external rewards. Should pupils be paid to attend class? Should they
be paid for successful completion of all or part of the pro-

gram? Some recent programs reflect the view that frequent additional incentives to learn are important to individual success, particularly with younger adults, and that cash bonuses for learning will provide a universally acceptable source of incentive.

Program evaluation and individual assessment can involve the use of tests. Measurement has been found to be least accurate among this adult group. Should tests be employed? For what purpose: to determine class placement, to find the diligent pupil, or to evaluate the program?

Since teaching adults to read is a new educational specialty with requisite skills yet to be determined, and since few teachers have been trained especially for this field, the question of who should teach adult illiterates arises. Should specific experiential and personal requirements be stated? In the absence of stated qualifications, elementary teachers are most often attracted to and are provided with the reading training skills for literacy training. These are not necessarily the most satisfactory teachers of adults. And since literacy training is a specialty, should exceptional teachers be given additional incentives to enter the area?

The form these issues have taken would seem to indicate the need for personal preferences or value judgments. Education, however, has often been called a *science*. Making choices that involve deciding which alternative is best is a constant occurrence in all sciences. Scientific investigation can help determine which preferences are not wise. Readers may, therefore, wish to change the form of the questions so that they more closely resemble testable hypotheses. This would not be an unreasonable procedure, since none of the issues mentioned has yet been the subject of research.

Program Management

The aims of instruction will need to be implemented through the development of a facilitative administrating structure. This structure will encompass both organizational roles and policies for decision making. Development of a sound program will probably necessitate incorporation of some existing organizational roles and customary policies for dealing with problems common to most educational institutions as well as some new roles and policies. Accommodating the administrative and procedural structure to the realities of a community's adult basic education needs may well be a trial-and-error process. There are, however, some activities that together may further the process of decision making.

1. *Keep adequate records.* Records that later may be used as the basis of program change should be accurate and complete. Test results, assessments, and behavioral descriptions should be included along with attendance records. Information about the pupil's place of original and previous educational experience is useful. Some time during the first few class weeks, after the pupil has accustomed himself to the class program, it is desirable to determine in an interview situation something of his family background and his general social adjustment in order to pinpoint and document possible future sources of difficulty that would tend to draw him away from the course. Medical records are also important sources of information. Dropouts and fadeouts should be interviewed to determine what caused them to lose interest in the program. An attempt should also be made to follow pupils after they have completed training to help determine the effect literacy has upon them. Good records aid in a policy of periodic program review and modification.

2. *Facilitate change.* Programs ought to be initiated with the consideration that they are experimental. Open-mindedness is necessary for innovation. Critical restraints to creative expressions by staff members should be removed.

3. *Recruit able teachers as adult literacy instructors.* Good teachers ought to be encouraged to become adult education instructors. Literacy instructors are specialists. To encour-

age teachers to enter this professional specialty it may be desirable to offer special incentives, such as additional compensation. Independent, cheerful, energetic, and patient instructors especially should be encouraged to become literacy teachers.

Good literacy instructors do not perform. To "perform" is taken to mean: to capture and hold the attention of a number of students, and to serve continuously as the mediator between the student and the information. This is the way teachers seem to define teaching (*Carlson, 1965*). Beyond this it would be difficult to make generalizations about the successful teacher. Good literacy instructors obviously need to be comfortable with adults.

4. *Promote inter-agency cooperation in literacy matters.* Efforts should be made to develop means of cooperation between literacy programs conducted in the same geographical areas. Information can be exchanged, plans and facilities coordinated. Agencies other than schools may also have an interest in basic education programs. Religious and private, but public-spirited, groups may also be simultaneously conducting literacy programs. Public and private organizations may be providing financial support to illiterate students. Literacy campaigns should be conducted on a community-wide basis to avoid animosity and competition to serve students. City or county literacy councils composed of all interested organizations might be established for this purpose.

Small school districts having limited available funds but wishing to establish literacy programs may find it convenient to develop joint programs with other districts in states where such sharing of materials, facilities, and instructors is not prohibited by law. Area councils could help interested districts to become aware of each other's program needs and policies.

Optimally, literacy programs should be established with the joint cooperation of federal, state, and local officials and all other interested agencies. Efficient use of Title IIb funds of the Elementary and Secondary Education Act of 1964 requires this coordinated effort.

Title IIb funds are designed to be used in three ways:

1. To assist local educational agencies in establishing programs and pilot projects.

2. To assist with the actual cost of adult education.

3. To assist state agencies in improving their technical and supervisory services to adult basic education.

For fiscal 1968, state aid to such programs will be matched by the federal government on a dollar-for-dollar basis. State education departments, however, have no direct influence over the management of many federally directed programs either primarily for the illiterate or that involve literacy training, for example, Community Action Programs (C.A.P.). Private, non-profit, and public agencies are eligible under C.A.P. for federal assistance. Funds for Community Action Programs need not be matched by the state government or by the agencies receiving them. These funds are not available to school districts.

Title IIa, together with IIIb of the Economic Opportunities Act of 1964, provides for Community Action Program Assistance for Migrant and Seasonal Farm workers. These programs are administered through state offices of the U.S. Office of Economic Opportunity.

Districts wishing to coordinate their basic education programs might seek the assistance of the Educational Advisory Service, which provides services and publications to aid in the improvement of sound educational practices, including materials and advice on organization, management, and financing of school systems. Advisory services are also provided on the construction of facilities, the methods of instruction, and the preparation of teachers. The Educational Advisory Service is an establishment of the U.S. Office of Education.

Program Coordination

Cooperation will not resolve all of the issues associated with facilitating the growth of literacy programs. While sound educational practice requires the cooperation of all agencies contributing to the basic education effort, sound educational management requires the coordination of all programs. Recruiting illiterate pupils has always been a major problem. Two or more programs may compete to serve adult illiterates. There are instances in large metropolitan areas where duplication services have been established but where many illiterates go unnoticed. Coordination of effort is a complex problem since decisions may involve agencies whose responsibilities cross state lines or whose responsibilities and authority are coextensive.

One means of establishing state-level coordination would be through the organization of a state council for literacy composed of the state superintendent of public instruction as an ex-officio member and representatives of: the U.S. Office of Education where U.S. Office Funds are utilized, the Department of Health, Education and Welfare where H.E.W. funds are involved, school districts having or planning adult basic education programs, and welfare agencies and private organizations contributing to local literacy programs.

A state-wide coordination group might include as one of its purposes the development of state-wide educational goals for the education of adult illiterates. Most states have developed educational plans for the education of adult non-readers. Many have curriculum manuals intended as guidelines for school districts. Examination of about two dozen different state curriculum guides indicates differences in thoroughness of planning and clarity of goals. The North Carolina program is an example of thorough planning for the education of rural illiterates. The New York State program is an exceptional example of planning for the urban adult illiterate. While curriculum guides are likely to influence the development of programs, particularly those initiated by school districts, such an effort is unilateral and may not represent all or even the best professional experience available.

Signs of Change

A recent study of adult basic education programs in the State of Illinois (*Greenleigh, 1965*) advised several interesting program modifications that may indicate the future courses of adult literacy programs generally. It was suggested that comprehensive adult education centers be developed to provide a wide range of educational experiences for both illiterates and their families, such as vocational training, job placement devices, and counseling. Residential programs could have therapeutic goals. Both illiterate parents and their children would temporarily move to "rehabilitation centers" outside their accustomed slum environments.

It was also suggested that day programs contemplating a "total educational experience" be established. A recurring problem in education is controlling experience outside the school that might influence in-school learning. Day programs would have the advantage of involving a large segment of the illiterates' waking time with a variety of culturally relevant activities.

Educational television might be introduced to support adult basic education. Previous experiments with educational television as the principal instruction medium have shown considerable problems. The use of television in the classroom as a support to other activities such as programmed texts or workbooks needs to be explored fully.

Teacher personnel issues also need to be resolved. Recommended were the development of training, the development of training facilities for adult education instructors, and the establishment of selected criteria and evaluation techniques to measure the ability of literacy instructors.

The intake of students should be routinized. Where no regular time for enrollment exists, class continuity and group organization are difficult. This is particularly so where materials are teacher-centered and the pupil is dependent on class presentations.

Many of these recommendations are similar to the armed forces literacy training in World War II: special training procedures, training of instructors, and regularized intake of students.

Even in well established programs pupils may be discouraged by a lag between the time they enroll and the time they are assigned to a class. Delay caused by the intake procedure should be minimal. Pre-program testing should include only those examinations which will quickly and accurately place a pupil in the program. Many pupils returning to school have vision and hearing problems. Pre-enrollment screening of vision and hearing is desirable where such examinations have not previously been conducted by physicians.

Placing the pupil into the program without delay helps minimize the chances that he will become a dropout or a fadeout. *Fadeouts,* or casual attendance, are a serious educational and social problem. Many adult pupils have irregular attendance habits as well as irregular work habits. Counselors will need to consider experimenting with follow-up procedures that will bring the fadeout back into a more active role in the program. Cooperation between case workers and the school may also be considered a desirable step.

Counseling the slow or exceptional student, whether by teacher or by a specially trained guidance worker, may help the critical adjustment-to-learning process and may also decrease the number of dropouts or fadeouts. Grouping students with physical handicaps serious enough to impede learning will encourage their progress. Pupils found to be exceptionally slow learners might be encouraged if they can be reorganized into separate groups.

• REFERENCES

BARNES. R. F. *Problems Facing Teachers and Administrators in Adult Basic Education Today.* A speech delivered to an assembly of adult basic education teachers in Chicago, April 3, 1965. In B. E.

Chapman (ed.), *Teaching Adults to Read, Basic Education Handbook*, Series I. Galien, Michigan: Allied Education Council, 1966.

CARLSON, R. O. *Adaptation of Educational Innovations*. Eugene, Oregon; The Center for the Advanced Study of Educational Administration, 1965.

GOLDBERG, S. *Army Training of Illiterates in World War II, Teach. Coll. Contr. Edu.*, 1951, No. 966.

GREENLEIGH ASSOCIATES, INC. *Educational Rehabilitation: An Evaluation of the Adult Basic Education Program of the State of Illinois*. New York: Greenleigh Associates, 1965.

LAND, C. "Social Research and Literacy Campaigns." *The International Review of Education*, 1963, 9, pp. 418–427.

NOYES, A.P., AND L. C. KOLB. *Modern Clinical Psychiatry*. Philadelphia: W. B. Saunders Company, 1963.

OETTINGER, L. *Physical Concomitants of Reading*. Claremont Reading Conference Yearbook, 1963.

WRIGHT, BEATRICE A. *Physical Disability—A Psychological Approach*. New York: Harper & Row, Publishers, 1960.

3

THE ADULT ILLITERATE AS A LEARNER

Adult illiterates are, first of all, adults in need of a basic education. Usually they are from culturally deprived environments. These two factors make them a fundamentally different population from that which the public school encounters ordinarily. Furthermore, adults cannot be compelled to attend school; nor will they be attracted to an institution whose use of authority is either arbitrary or without appeal. There seems to be no question that to benefit illiterates it is important to teach them specific skills and knowledge. However, these educational experiences must conform to the needs of citizens who already have established roles within the community. Two topics are discussed in this chapter: the social climate of poverty, particularly as it influences the adult illiterate, and the adult as a student.

• THE CULTURE OF POVERTY

The culture of poverty is characterized by: (1) a unique relationship between its members and the society at large; (2) the nature of the slum (whether urban or rural); (3) the nature of the family; and (4) the value, character structure, and attitudes of the individual.

Oscar Lewis, noted authority on the culture of the urban and rural poor, has stated in a recent article (*1966*) that among the poor there is both a disengagement from the activities characteristic of the larger society and widespread hostility toward all basic social institutions, which are regarded as machinations of the dominant middle class. The adult illiterate, as a participant in what Lewis identifies as a lower-class culture, can neither communicate with nor fully comprehend the middle-class society. He cannot participate knowledgeably in public affairs because he does not have access to varied opinions and facts. His range of economic choice is limited to what he has observed and what has been communicated to him by word of mouth. His knowledge of geography is limited to information either imparted orally by others or discovered through his own travels.

Many of the habits of the poor who identify with this group will interfere with the development of communication skills. They do not participate in the social institutions that would benefit them most. They are suspicious of the motives of the police. They do not belong to labor organizations. They do not use banks. However, they are familiar with the army, jails, and public welfare. For lack of ready cash the poor make frequent small purchases at neighborhood stores where prices are notoriously inflated. Since they are poor and without a regular income they must borrow at usurious rates. They regard institutions of the middle class with feelings of suspicion, fear, and anger. Representatives of organized religion and government are not trusted. Clashes with authority are common and range over the entire continuum of socially obstructive activity — from a mild protest such as refusal to pay the rent, to violent exchanges like the now familiar burnings, lootings and assaults, where many people are injured or bullied.

There is widespread awareness of middle-class values and even approval of them, but these values are seldom applied. Marriage is avoided as an entangling alliance that would be difficult and expensive to break. Divorce also requires inter-action with officialdom. Marriage does not provide economic security because typically neither spouse is dependably em-ployed and because property other than personal effects is seldom involved. As a result, fatherless homes are common. Where there are several children, competition for parental affection and recognition is keen even though the rewards are customarily meagre.

Such home conditions frequently bring about sex-role con-fusions. The lower-class male is preoccupied with his masculinity, even at an early age. He is uncertain of himself and his relations with others, but, ironically, the belief is widespread that males are superior.

Among men, school attendance may be interpreted as a sign of weakness, particularly in circumstances where both men and women might attend together. However, the experience of recently established literacy programs has been that an al-most equal proportion of men and women are attracted to class (*Otto and Ford, 1966*). Why this is so has not been established. One reason may be that new programs and new materials designed especially for adults are less likely to be oriented around child-centered interests.

Lewis notes that while the community of the poor is highly gregarious, it is without permanent organizations of its own. The lower class culture is, in its lack of structure, unlike even the post-primitive societies. From it spring individuals who have a "strong feeling of fatalism, helplessness, dependence and inferiority" (*Lewis, 1966*). The culture of poverty is not peculiar to one racial group. These traits are shared by poor Negroes, Spanish-Americans, and whites alike.

• EDUCATION FOR SOCIAL CHANGE

Education should bring about the establishment of a social dialogue between the illiterate and the culture. Through the process of education and the content of reading materials introduced in the classroom he can learn about his society and, in turn, the society can learn about him. Outsiders do not evoke confidence easily. The teacher's role ideally situates him to learn about the illiterate's problems and needs. An interchange of information is as important to the teacher as a social action representation of society is to the student. In this way educators can also learn where educational procedures and goals need to be modified to fit the social and psychological needs of the socially deprived.

Most important, the culturally deprived illiterate adult must be considered as an adult member of the community. The psychological differences between adults and children create special problems for education. The more important group characteristics of adults are considered next.

• THE ADULT LEARNER

To no one's surprise, adults have been shown to be different from children on a variety of psychological measures. Consideration of these differences is important in the planning of educational experiences.

Intelligence as a Function of Age

Certain ideas about age differences are held by almost everyone. Youngsters are believed to be quicker, more imaginative, more radical, and more impulsive. Older people are supposed to have superior judgment and more stability, but they also seem slower and more conservative. These common beliefs about individual differences bear some relationship to fact.

A variety of studies point to lower intelligence in older people. Tests of spatial relations and reasoning are particularly indicative of differences between adults in their early twenties and adults in early middle age — say, in their thirties. Part of the difference in test scores between older and younger groups may be a result of the way the studies were conducted. Age differences were represented by different individuals in different age groups. Some relatively recent investigations have followed a particular group through many years. One such study was of men recruited into the army during World War I. Another was of a large group of gifted children in the 1920's. These longitudinal studies indicate that if there is intellectual and social stimulation many people will increase their ability to solve problems. A decrease in intellectual powers seems not to be inevitable; among the very old are many highly intelligent individuals, indicating that, as Tyler (*1965*) says, "individual differences are very great and they often outweigh the effects of age. . . ."

Personality as a Function of Age

One important conclusion to be drawn from interest tests given to adult subjects of all ages is that interests established in the early twenties will ordinarily be the prevailing interests of middle age. But there are also some behavioral changes that occur as a function of age. Older men tend to be less dominant. Older people, generally, tend to be more anxious and intolerant. This may in part be attributable to physical illness and the consequent breakdown of social contacts. The maintenance of social ties, both within and outside of the family, and a healthy attitude towards one's self and the future augur well for adjustment, as do interest in employment and hobbies. Adult education can contribute to the maintenance of social ties and interest in a vocation. These contacts with the world help prevent internal stress and tensions.

Changes in Ability Due to Age

All types of measureable skills tend to decline after the age of 30; but although *average* ability declines, there are great differences in skill proficiencies at any age level.

Visual efficiency declines steadily with age, particularly after age 50. Increasing illumination seems to improve the performance of older people more than that of younger ones. Physical strength also declines. The decrease is gradual, so that the difference between males age 20 and 60 is less than 20 percent. Learning rate is not accurately predicted by measures of intelligence, which have been discussed previously. However, older people learn a little less readily than younger ones. This difference is particularly apparent where old habits interfere with the development of new ones.

Memory is also impaired by age, though the type of task used to measure memory often determines the amount of impairment. Complex skills such as those involving a combination of manipulatory movements, perception and cognition are accomplished in different ways by older people. The older person distributes his time differently. He spends more time thinking about what he is going to do. Where modifications of performance are necessary, older people tend to make the same errors more often.

Developmental States

One way of looking at the difficulties imposed on the educational system by the need to educate adults is to observe the changing demands made by the society on the individual throughout his life span. Among the more primitive cultures change in familial and tribal obligations is almost as inevitably associated with youth, maturity and old age as the biological processes themselves. The ritualistic tasks commonly found within these societal arrangements are not only the means by which the person is accommodated and assimilated by the society, but also the vehicle through which he discovers individuality. Each maturation level has its own unique conflicts as part of the process of social and biological change. The cultural dynamics — that is, how society organizes to meet the challenges of the environment — determine the nature and intensity of the change process for the individual.

Descriptions of the process and the product of change can

help the teacher of adults understand and plan for educationally significant differences. For these we look to several authorities. Investigators from the University of Vienna have identified and studied three aspects of the process, termed by them *Lebenslauf* or "Course of Life." These are: (1) the productivity at each stage, (2) the activities and events characteristic of each stage, and (3) the interexperiences at each stage. The idea of *life stages* has been developed from the work of Frenkel, Buhler, and Havighurst. Each stage is seen by these students of individual differences as having characteristically different tendencies and dominant needs. Erikson, a psychoanalytically oriented psychologist, has been more interested in describing the process of change from the standpoint of the individual. He terms the stages in this process "life challenges." The challenge of adolescence is identity versus identity diffusion; the challenge of young adulthood is intimacy versus isolation; the challenge of middle life is a generativity versus self-absorption; and the challenge of old age is integrity versus despair. Each stage of life is conceptualized by all of these investigators as qualitatively different from every other. Individuals assume new interrelationships with one another as they age. The traits and activities appropriate to one age are at variance with those of any other age.

• ADULT EDUCATION—A MODEL FOR PLANNED CHANGE

There are historic as well as psychological reasons for considering the organization and goals of adult basic education as somewhat different from those of elementary and secondary education. The education of adults has a deep-rooted tradition of its own. It began in nineteenth-century Scandinavia as a product of democratic and religious humanism at a time when "culture" separated the affluent from the poor, who were denied what we now would consider fundamental human dignity. New schools had to be developed to make representa-tive democracy feasible by crossing social, economic and political barriers. People's universities, called *Folk High Schools,* were established. Their purpose was to bring together the intellectual and the common man, not only to convey knowledge to the poor — the cultural have-nots — but also to share the problems of everyday life and confront these difficulties with wisdom and humanity. Primarily through this means an "organic" culture was eventually developed in which any adult, regardless of class, could participate.

Adult education has been the working man's hope for changing his place in the social class structure. It has also become an accepted means of self-improvement. These goals are often, but not necessarily, inconsistent. Throughout Western Europe and the United States adult education has from its inception been a means of establishing a dialogue between the individual and the society. The school communicates the culture; the individual communicates his needs.

The adult illiterate returning to school is faced with the disadvantages of his age, his social background and, often, an educational organization not designed to accommodate him. Public schools usually find that organizing classes for adult non-readers creates unique problems. Teachers having the requisite training for basic reading instruction are usually neither trained to nor interested in teaching adults. Methods that work best with youngsters are not necessarily appropriate for instructing mature individuals. Teachers accustomed to the broad developmental goals of instruction that characterize primary reading and language arts in the elementary school may find specific goals of instruction restrictive. Materials used to teach children to read have not been found satisfactory for instructing adults (see Chapter 4 for a full discussion of this problem), just as the loosely knit organization of adult literacy classes is not appropriate to the education of children. Children require much more structured learning activities than adults. The free interchanges between literacy instructor and pupil that are characteristic of adult-to-adult social interaction are often not expedient in the instruction of youth.

While the broad developmental goals of public school education are necessarily less precise, they present a finite task in the sense that education is usually conceived of as ending at age 18 or with the completion of high school. Adult education, however, is a lifelong effort, a continuing process of social and intellectual accomplishment in which both the concomitants of age and the degree of intellectual competence determine the student's direction of effort. An educational institution that is designed to accommodate students with differing educational achievement, differing ages and differing needs and that also plans its educational experiences in consideration of what is known about these differences will be more likely to retain its adult, marginally literate pupils.

• REFERENCES

LEWIS, O. "The Culture of Poverty." *Scientific American,* 1965, Vol. 215, pp. 19–25.

OTTO, W., AND D. FORD. Paper read at the National Reading Conference, St. Petersburg, Florida, December, 1966.

TYLER, L. *The Psychology of Human Differences* (3rd Ed.). New York: Appleton-Century-Crofts, 1965.

4 MATERIALS FOR TEACHING ADULTS TO READ

The five lists of materials that follow in this chapter are limited to those useful in developing students' reading skills to the point where they can progress independently. Some writers have called this initial stage of reading development simply "the introductory stage" (*Hayes, Lighthall and Lupton, 1964*). Smith and Smith (*1962*) have referred to it as the level where the "mechanics of reading" are taught. Other writers prefer to describe this stage in terms of grade levels of accomplishment.

The reviewers felt, however, that grade level was neither an important nor necessarily a useful concept, even though its abandonment creates some obvious evaluation problems. It is appropriate, therefore, to explain why grade levels recommended, whether by the publisher or by an independent source such as another author, were not considered and why evaluations were not put in these terms.

In defining level of reading difficulty, "grade" is most often thought of in terms of a sequence of tasks to be accomplished and the linguistic restraints imposed upon reading materials. Thus, task *B*, a competency assigned to the second grade, is taught after task *A* and before task *C*, which are assigned to the first and third grades respectively. Likewise, short sentences and short, frequently encountered words are used, reflecting the reading, linguistic and psychological limitations of children.

Readability level is usually determined by a complicated

formula (*Dale and Chall, 1948; Spache, 1953*), part of which has reference to "easy" and "hard" words. Difficulty levels of words are determined by whether they are or are not included on a "standard" list. The most common standard lists are (1) the Dale (*1931*) list of 769 words common to both the International Kindergarten Union list (*1928*) and the Lorge *Teacher's Word Book* (*1921*) first thousand words, and (2) the Dale list of 3,000 words (*Dale and Chall, 1948*). Frequency counts made from one collection of materials will differ from those made from another, as Mitzel (*1965*) has demonstrated.

Mitzel selected materials adults actually read as the basis of her word count. She chose selections from material issued by the federal and local governments, newspapers, application blanks, store signs, menus, the Yellow Pages, comic books, general advertising literature, union literature, and religious tracts. Hers was not an accidental choice of sources, but a selection made from personal observations and interviews. She found that there was only a 66% overlap between her 5,000 word list and the first 5,000 words on the Lorge-Thorndike 30,000 word list. This raises the question of what criterion ought to be used for selecting materials in making frequency counts. Lists based on children's reading and children's conceptual needs, as Thorndike and Lorge and Mitzel have recognized, will have different constituency from those based on adult needs.

Level of reading difficulty is also thought of in terms of the linguistic restraints imposed by immaturity. Short written sentences reflect the inability of children to use or comprehend involved sentence structure. However, sentence length itself is not known to be a restraining factor for adults, even culturally disadvantaged adults.

Reading grade level as a criterion of difficulty facilitates one kind of comparison between reading programs, just as the assignment of grade level of ability aids the teacher in determining how far the individual pupil has progressed in the developmental sequence. That it is an artifact has been demonstrated in the previous paragraphs. But as a standard criterion whereby all programs may be compared and as a means for making normative judgments about pupil progress, it has considerable utility for adult programs.

There are two importunate and unmet needs for the development of modern adult basic reading programs. First, materials from all sources should be capable of being integrated. Convenience demands that there be a common yardstick for comparison. Second, standardized adult reading tests based on adult reading needs should be developed not only to facilitate entrance into adult educational programs, which is of particular importance to adult basic educators, but also to determine the level of reading competency in the adult population. Both needs are contingent in part upon the development of an unambiguous sequence of adequately described and, therefore, measurable adult reading behaviors.

• PROCEDURES USED FOR COLLECTING MATERIALS

A list of publishers was compiled from several sources: the 1966 edition of _Textbooks in Print,_ bibliographies supplied by nearly 500 school districts having adult basic education programs, and the resources of the Instructional Materials Center of the University of Wisconsin.

All publishers on the compiled list were polled. Three questions were asked: (1) Did they publish materials which they would recommend for the adult basic literacy market? (2) Did they intend to publish materials for this market in the future? If the answer to either question 1 or 2 was yes, (3) would they furnish the Center with descriptive literature, etc.? Many companies responded with complimentary copies of their materials.

When inspection of descriptive information and/or actual materials led to a decision to do a detailed analysis of materials, the materials were purchased through regular commercial channels. All were obtained through a local book-store. One reason for this was to determine the availability of materials in a manner similar to that which schools might employ. Inordinate delays, on the order of two or three months, would cast considerable doubt on the utility of a particular selection. For this purpose, partially filled orders can be considered as important as unfilled ones.

In choosing materials to be examined, considerable reliance was placed on the publishers' claims that their materials were useful for adult basic education. However, some materials obviously intended for the elementary school market were eliminated on the basis of descriptions and pictures furnished by the publisher.

• WHY AN ADULT EDUCATION CHECK LIST?

Any description of materials leaves much to be desired in determining their utility. Utility, it turns out, is situationally relevant. On the other hand, we wish to make a variety of types of information and opinion available, all or some part of which might facilitate program development. Accompanying each program notation and description, therefore, is the *Check List to Evaluate Adult Basic Reading Materials.* Its purpose is briefly and systematically to present facts common to each program and evaluative statements consensually arrived at by the reviewers. Thus, each program can be compared with every other program in a substantial number of ways. Briefly, then, these are the concerns reflected by the *Check List:*

Do the materials contribute to the widely held feeling among adult illiterates that "school is for kids"?

The reviewers took the stand that with few exceptions materials that reflect childhood interests would have little appeal to adults. They are, therefore, generally not reviewed and not listed.

*Was important informational content being conveyed
through the practice selections while reading skills were
being learned?*

The primary use of language, for both readers and non-
readers, is as a means of conducting social interactions. Social
"meanings" are relatively imprecise though necessarily complex. The non-reader requires some training in using both
oral and written language for the specilized nonsocial purpose
of transmitting and receiving information to be used in and
of itself.

From the psychological standpoint, learning to use language
in a new way is but one aspect of adjustment to a new or
relatively unusual role — that of student. From a psycho-
linguistic point of view, the student — as opposed to any
other person with the exception of teacher — is required to
adapt himself to some rather strict language bounds both in
the magnitude and in the precision of his utterances.

There is at least one other reason for using basic reading
instruction to convey information. The changing relationship of many, if not most, illiterates from nonparticipating —
that is, nonfunctioning — social members to self-sustaining,
responsible citizens requires both social experimentation with
personally rewarding outcomes and new information about
society. It is a reasonable and economical educational procedure to combine the kinds of information that will help
the individual act efficiently not only as a student (i.e., as a
user of precise language and a user of particular reading
skills) but also as an adult citizen. An illustration of the
kind of material that might be incorporated into a content
and skill reading task is found in two newspapers, *The Pacemaker* and *City Challenge,* published by the Detroit Public
Schools. The front page of Volume 1, Number 1, of *The
Pacemaker* includes four articles and/or article leads on the
following subjects: the high cost of living, the upcoming
election in Michigan, legal obligations of citizens, and telephone numbers to use when various types of assistance are

required. Characteristic of all four articles are (1) readability, (2) factual orientation, including dates, telephone numbers, and references to specific laws and various amounts of money, and (3) citizenship information content.

How is the new pupil incorporated into the program and at what point in the program sequence does he enter?

Do all students have to begin at one place and go through the same sequence of lessons? Standardized adult reading tests are being developed by various private and public agencies. Until means are found to relate programs to these instruments, each program must have its own entry test, which can be used accurately and rapidly to place students with materials that are best suited to their level of accomplishment.

It is not uncommon, for example, to find illiterates who have learned to recognize some sounds in isolation but who cannot synthesize the separate sound elements into a word. This developmental block is frequently accompanied by strong affect and signs of personality disruption. Therefore, analytic skills should probably not be emphasized in the early stages of instruction, if at all.

What is the source of vocabulary that the program introduces?

Vocabulary is one means educators have of comparing programs in the absence of grade-level criteria. When considering the merits of a particular program, it is important to know not only the total size of the vocabulary introduced, in terms of the source used, but also the rate, in terms of the amount of practice, at which words are introduced.

Does the program contain enough practice materials?

One of the most frequently voiced criticisms of adult literacy programs is that reading skills and vocabulary are introduced too rapidly. Adult illiterates have not learned how to learn, so retention is likely to be poor. They are, in fact inefficient learners who require considerably more exposures to skill than school children of comparable ability. Provision for overlearning reading skills may be as important as the way the skills are introduced. Therefore, workbooks and exercises should be constructed that provide for the needs of even the more inept learners.

How is progress assessed?

Adults who have a history of educational failure tend to perform poorly on examinations. It is, therefore, desirable to make evaluation an intrinsic part of the program. It is important also that pupils see how well they are doing and that such evaluation be frequent because the pupil who has previously failed will tend to be discouraged easily and often.

Are other language arts skills taught in conjunction with reading?

Reading is not an isolated skill. Appropriate writing, spelling and speech practice should be provided to reinforce learned reading habits, and all should be taught in well integrated units.

How does the pupil gain self-reliance and self-respect?

While most authorities agree that it is necessary for the illiterate to have frequent encouragement from teachers, it is also desirable for him to rapidly develop independence from the judgment of others (note *Skinner, 1954*). If programs depend on group participation for their success, group work should be directed toward stimulating the individual without inhibiting the slow or indifferent learners, who need special encouragement.

What provisions have been made to test the materials previous to their being offered for sale?

The sequence of material development should include a trial stage that includes the participation of an audience essentially similar to that for which the program is contemplated. By way of example, materials designed to teach English as a second literate language have been used in adult basic education programs. But the non-reader and the non-reader of English differ in motivation and academic ability. Literates have learned how to learn through written language and how to be successful students. Such materials, may be appropriate for one group but not for the other.

Different types of materials require different provisions for adequate try-out. Programmed materials require highly specific kinds of responses. Goals are operational. It is, therefore, possible to use a relatively small population for testing purposes. Trying new materials should, perhaps, include consideration of some of the less easily systematized variables such as pupil interest and enjoyment and ease of use. Materials that have been designed for and tested on a particular audience should also be revised according to the experimental findings.

Has the material been published with some consideration for the audience?

The following aspects of printed materials have often been neglected by publishers. *Type face* should be pleasing and contribute to the learning process. The *individual page* should not be cluttered and distracting, but simple and distraction free. *Paper* should not yellow and turn brittle rapidly. The pages of *adequately bound books* will not tear free with hard use.

Are there illustrations that facilitate instruction?

Beginning reading materials employ illustrations in a variety of ways. They can help communicate in general what a passage or story is about, they can portray specific incidents, and they can also dramatize new words presented in the unit. The relevancy of particular illustrations depends largely on the way lesson materials are intended to be utilized. Where class discussion is planned as a means for introducing content, pertinent illustrations may serve to help the teacher organize his presentation. Where students work independently, illustrations that aid in either developing vocabulary or obtaining meaning from relatively difficult passages are most appropriate.

Do the manuals describe the program in detail?

Appropriate contents will depend partly on the nature of the program. Some information is particularly useful to the teacher: the author's organizational plan, teaching methods that have been found particularly successful with the material, and, where the teacher is to play a major part in instruction, complete and specific lesson plans.

• ORGANIZATION OF CONTENTS

Reading programs are described in List I, which is arranged alphabetically according to publisher. Supplementary skill building and reading practice materials are listed separately by topic in List II and List III. Other materials that may be useful are given without annotations: List IV names U.S. Government Printing Office Publications, and List V includes materials for teaching reading to foreign-born adults. A selected list of recent professional books is also included in List VI, which is limited to publications that will be helpful to all teachers of adult illiterates. Some of these publications contain background information, while others detail specific techniques of instruction. Publishers' addresses are given at the end of this chapter.

• REFERENCES

THE CHILD STUDY COMMITTEE OF THE INTERNATIONAL KINDERGARTEN UNION. *A Study of the Vocabulary of Children before Entering the First Grade.* Washington: The International Kindergarten Union, 1928.

DALE, EDGAR, AND JEANNE S. CHALL. A formula for predicting readability. *Educational Research Bulletin,* 1948, 27, 11–20 and 37–54.

HAYES, ANN, NANCY LIGHTHALL, AND DAN LUPTON. *An Investigation of Materials and Methods for the Introductory Stage of Adult*

Literacy Education. Chicago: Adult Education Council of Greater Chicago, 1964.

MITZEL, M. ADELE. "The Functional Reading Word List for Adults." *Adult Education,* Winter, 1966, pp. 67–69.

SKINNER, B. F. "The Science of Learning and the Art of Teaching." *Harvard Educational Review,* 1954, 24, 86–97.

SMITH, EDWIN M. AND MARIE P. *Teaching Reading to Adults.* Washington, D.C.: National Association of Public School Adult Educators, 1962.

SPACHE, GEORGE. "A New Readability Formula for Primary-Grade Reading Materials." *Elementary School Journal,* 1953, 53, 410–413.

THORNDIKE, EDWARD L., AND IRVING LORGE. *The Teacher's Word Book of 30,000 Words.* New York: Columbia University, 1944.

Textbooks in Print 1966. New York: R. R. Bowker Company, 1966.

LIST I
Basic Reading Programs for Adults

Included here are programs for teaching basic reading skills to adults, listed by publisher. A completed *Check List to Evaluate Adult Reading Materials* follows each system. The complete *Check List* includes 50 items; but certain of the items are not applicable with all systems, so in practice the lists range from 30-odd to 50 items. The complete *Check List* is given first for information purposes. Publishers' addresses are given after List VI.

· *Check List to Evaluate Adult Basic Reading Materials*

YES NO 1. materials have an adult appearance

YES NO 2. covers mark the owners as illiterates

YES NO 3. contents reflect adult tastes and interests

YES NO 4. contents reflect adult basic education need for acculturation and re-socialization

YES NO 5. presents problems of social maintenance as filling in forms, keeping accounts, making time purchases

YES NO 6. presents citizenship or civic responsibility content

YES NO 7. presents problems of social adjustment

YES NO 8. presents special information such as technical content suitable for specific trades or job descriptions

YES NO 9. suitable for English as a second literate language class

YES NO 10. placement test(s) included in materials

YES NO 11. placement test easily administered

YES NO 12. placement test quickly places individual into materials at appropriate level of difficulty

YES NO 13. materials programed

YES NO 14. includes practice reading materials

YES NO 15. practice readings are short

YES NO 16. practice reading includes comprehension questions

YES NO 17. failure in program difficult

YES NO 18. sequentially organized skill building

YES NO 19. includes phonic skill training

YES NO 20. includes context skill training

YES NO 21. includes word analysis skills by word form

YES NO 22. includes dictionary skills

YES NO 23. includes other fact locating skills such as reading telephone directories

YES NO 24. includes map or graph reading training

YES NO 25. includes list of vocabulary introduced

YES NO 26. vocabulary taken from a standard frequency list such as the Lorge or Mitzel list

YES NO 27. vocabulary list analyzed according to frequency by standard list, i.e., how many taken from 1st 400, etc.

YES NO 28. includes teaching manual

YES NO 29. manual includes lesson plans

YES NO 30. manual includes teaching methods

YES NO 31. manual describes organization of material

YES NO 32. provides means for self-evaluation
YES NO 33. self-evaluation is frequent
YES NO 34. self-evaluation is part of learning program
YES NO 35. includes handwriting training and practice
YES NO 36. includes speech training and practice
YES NO 37. pupil works mainly by himself with minimum of teacher help
YES NO 38. group work supports the effort of individual
YES NO 39. materials have been field tested
YES NO 40. population upon which materials tested is described
YES NO 41. results of field testing are reported
YES NO 42. materials have been revised according to results of field testing
YES NO 43. illustrations augment instruction
YES NO 44. illustrations are tasteful
YES NO 45. illustrations are clearly and unambiguously related to text
YES NO 46. materials are durable
YES NO 47. materials are inexpensive
YES NO 48. materials are consumable
YES NO 49. style of type is pleasing
YES NO 50. layout design is pleasing

· *Affiliated Publishers, Inc.*

· First Steps in Reading English, 1959
  Christine M. Gibson and I. A. Richards

This is a linguistic, unprogramed series. The introduction of sounds, symbols, words, and sentence types is carefully controlled. Handwriting is neither taught nor required in the exercises. The materials were written for children, but they should be palatable to adults.

First Steps is a series of four books with workbooks. At the beginning of the series short sentences, using a limited number of letters, are introduced in conjunction with stick figure drawings. Very gradually the student is introduced to more letters through other words and to more sentence patterns. Exact sentence meaning is taught by making the sentences verifiable through action pictures.

After the student studies a lesson, he draws the picture in the workbook that the directions — using the same words that he has studied in the book — call for. Therefore, in a rather painless way the student's comprehension of the sentences he has read in the books is checked.

Four filmstrips are correlated with the lessons in the four books and workbooks. They may be used as review or as introductory material for the lessons in the books because they contain the same sentences.

YES	1.	materials have an adult appearance
NO	2.	covers mark the owners as illiterates
NO	3.	contents reflect adult tastes and interests
NO	4.	contents reflect adult basic education need for ac-culturation and re-socialization
NO	5.	presents problems of social maintenance as filling in forms, keeping accounts, making time purchases
NO	6.	presents citizenship or civic responsibility content
NO	7.	presents problems of social adjustment
NO	8.	presents special information such as technical content suitable for specific trades or job descriptions
YES	9.	suitable for English as a second literate language class
NO	10.	placement test(s) included in materials
NO	13.	materials programed
YES	14.	includes practice reading materials
YES	15.	practice readings are short
YES	16.	practice reading includes comprehension questions
NO	17.	program difficult for adults
YES	18.	sequentially organized skill building
NO	19.	includes phonic skill training
NO	20.	includes context skill training

YES 21. includes word analysis skills by word form
NO   22. includes dictionary skills
NO   23. includes other fact locating skills such as reading telephone directories
NO   24. includes map or graph reading training
YES 25. includes list of vocabulary introduced
NO   26. vocabulary taken from a standard frequency list such as the Lorge or Mitzel list
NO   28. includes teaching manual
YES 32. provides means for self-evaluation
YES 33. self-evaluation is frequent
YES 34. self-evaluation is part of learning program
NO   35. includes handwriting training and practice
NO   36. includes speech training and practice
YES 37. pupil words mainly by himself with minimum of teacher help
NO   38. group work supports the effort of individual
NO   39. materials have been field tested
YES 43. illustrations augment instruction
YES 44. illustrations are tasteful
YES 45. illustrations are clearly and unambiguously related to text
YES 46. materials are durable
YES 47. materials are inexpensive
YES 48. materials are consumable
YES 49. style of type is pleasing
YES 50. layout design is pleasing

The Allied Education Council

- THE MOTT BASIC LANGUAGE SKILLS PROGRAM, 1966
  BYRON E. CHAPMAN AND LOUIS SCHULZ

The program is a phonics-linguistic approach, with the emphasis upon individual reading and writing rather than group work. The time recommended for completion of the beginning basic skill program is 60 hours for *300A* and 60 hours for

300B. The complete program extends through the twelfth-grade level.

Basic Language Skills — 300A

Although cursive writing practice is first taught to familiarize the students with the alphabet, handwriting practice is scattered throughout the 300 Series.

Consonant and blend sounds are taught through use of sample words associated with photographs. The short vowels are presented in word families, which the student reads orally and writes. Some essential rules of grammar are taught deductively. Sample forms are included to give the students practice in everyday reading and writing situations, such as filling out application blanks and checks. The book is concluded with a story several paragraphs in length followed by comprehension questions.

Basic Language Skills — 300B

Vowel diagraphs, followed by long vowel sounds, are taught by the same procedure as the short vowel sounds in *300A.* The major change in *300B* is the frequent inclusion of reading selections several paragraphs in length with comprehension questions. Likewise, grammatical rules receive more emphasis. Fewer photographs are used, so that the students are forced to depend on reading alone for meaning.

Word Bank — 300

The *Word Bank* is a collection of photographs of 200 objects familiar to most adults. The printed name of each object — in upper and lower case manuscript and in cursive — is taught by association. Spelling tests are included for each 25-word unit. The book is optional in the 300 Series program.

Instruction Manual — Series 300

In addition to practical suggestions on how to introduce new material and how to handle classroom problems, the manual includes lesson plans for *300A* and *300B*. Once the pattern of procedure is established, the lesson plans are less extensive, consisting mainly of enrichment activities.

Teaching Adults to Read

This is a supplementary orientation book for the inexperienced teacher of adults at the beginning level of basic skills development. Both methodological and sociological-psychological considerations are discussed. A list of enrichment materials available from other commercial sources and placement and diagnostic tests are also included.

YES	1.	materials have an adult appearance
NO	2.	covers mark the owners as illiterates
YES	3.	contents reflect adult tastes and interests
NO	4.	contents reflect adult basic education need for acculturation and re-socialization
YES	5.	presents problems of social maintenance as filling in forms, keeping accounts, making time purchases
NO	6.	presents citizenship or civic responsibility content
NO	7.	presents problems of social adjustment
NO	8.	presents special information such as technical content suitable for specific trades or job descriptions
NO	9.	suitable for English as a second literate language class
YES	10.	placement test(s) included in materials
YES	11.	placement test easily administered
YES	12.	placement test quickly places individual into materials at appropriate level of difficulty
NO	13.	materials programed
YES	14.	includes practice reading materials
YES	15.	practice readings are short
NO	16.	practice reading includes comprehension questions
NO	17.	program difficult for adults
YES	18.	sequentially organized skill building
YES	19.	includes phonic skill training

NO   20. includes context skill training
YES 21. includes word analysis skills by word form
NO   22. includes dictionary skills
NO   23. includes other fact locating skills such as reading telephone directories
NO   24. includes map or graph reading training
YES 25. includes list of vocabulary introduced
YES 26. vocabulary taken from a standard frequency list such as Lorge or Mitzel list
NO   27. vocabulary list analyzed accordingly to frequency by standard list, i.e., how many taken from 1st 500, etc.
YES 28. includes teaching manual
YES 29. manual includes lesson plans
YES 30. manual includes teaching methods
YES 31. manual describes organization of material
NO   32. provides means for self-evaluation
YES 35. includes handwriting training and practice
NO   36. includes speech training and practice
YES 37. pupil works mainly by himself with minimum of teacher help
NO   38. group work supports the effort of individual
YES 39. materials have been field tested
NO   40. population upon which materials tested is described
NO   41. results of field testing are reported
YES 42. materials have been revised according to results of field testing
YES 43. illustrations augment instruction
YES 44. illustrations are tasteful
YES 45. illustrations are clearly and unambiguously related to text
YES 46. materials are durable
YES 47. materials are inexpensive
YES 48. materials are consumable
NO   49. style of type is pleasing
NO   50. layout design is pleasing

• *American Incentive to Read*

• AMERICAN INCENTIVE TO READ MATERIALS, 1965

These materials include workbook-type exercises and coordinated phonograph records. Although a teacher is required to start the lessons, the student learns the letter sounds through the records, which provide dialectical uniformity. The estimated time for completing the program is 125 hours.

S.P.A.C.E. Test

This diagnostic test — *Structural Phonics Affecting Comprehension of English* — is intended to be given at the beginning of the program to determine the student's weaknesses in phonics skills. An *Examiner's Copy* is also available, with directions for administration and scoring. Matrices may be obtained to facilitate scoring.

Student Text, Books 1 and 2

At the initial stage, short vowels are studied in simple words that require combination with only the regular consonants. A small number of sight words is also taught. Small drawings are used to introduce new letter sounds; the initial letter of the object name has the sound. The sound is enunciated by the teacher and then by records; finally the student sees it printed in his book.

Teaching Text

Besides providing detailed lesson plans, the teaching text includes an outline of good practices for the untrained teacher.

Student Supplement

The supplement includes five progress tests in phonics skills, the first two of which are administered by records to equalize the students' chances for success until they become accustomed to the instructor's speech. Scoring and evaluation services are available for a fee, or the tests may be scored by the instructor. A _Dictionary of Sounds_ is also included, with drawings and examples of words containing the variety of sounds for each letter and diagraph. The record and page number where the material was originally taught is included.

Record Album

The set of 24 correlated records is an integral part of the program.

NO 1. materials have an adult appearance

NO 2. covers mark the owners as illiterates

NO 3. contents reflect adult tastes and interests

NO 4. contents reflect adult basic education need for acculturation and re-socialization

NO 5. presents problems of social maintenance as filling in forms, keeping accounts, making time purchases

NO 6. presents citizenship or civic responsibility content

NO 7. presents problems of social adjustment

NO 8. presents special information such as technical content suitable for specific trades or job descriptions

NO 9. suitable for English as a second literate language class

YES 10. placement test (s) included in materials

YES 11. placement test easily administered

YES 12. placement test quickly places individual into materials at appropriate level of difficulty

NO 13. materials programed

YES 14. includes practice reading materials

YES 15. practice readings are short

NO 16. practice reading includes comprehension questions

NO 17. program difficult for adults

YES 18. sequentially organized skill building

YES 19. includes phonic skill training

NO 20. includes context skill training

NO 21. includes word analysis skills by word form

NO 22. includes dictionary skills

NO 23. includes other fact locating skills such as reading telephone directories

NO 24. includes map or graph reading training

NO 25. includes list of vocabulary introduced

NO 26. vocabulary taken from a standard frequency list such as the Lorge or Mitzel list

YES 28. includes teaching manual

YES 29. manual includes lesson plans

YES 30. manual includes teaching methods

YES 31. manual describes organization of material

YES 32. provides means for self-evaluation

NO 33. self-evaluation is frequent

NO 34. self-evaluation is part of learning program

NO 35. includes handwriting training and practice

NO 36. includes speech training and practice

YES 37. pupil works mainly by himself with minimum of teacher help

NO 38. group work supports the effort of individual

YES 39. materials have been field tested

NO 40. population upon which materials tested is described

NO 41. results of field testing are reported

NO 42. materials have been revised according to results of field testing

YES 43. illustrations augment instruction

YES 44. illustrations are tasteful

NO 45. illustrations are clearly and unambiguously related to text

YES 46. materials are durable

NO 47. materials are inexpensive

NO 48. materials are consumable

YES 49. style of type is pleasing

YES 50. layout design is pleasing

• *Behavioral Research Laboratories*

• READING, SERIES I, 1966
  M. W. SULLIVAN

Reading, Series I, consists of four consumable workbooks, four correlated readers, a placement test and a teacher's guide. Teachers may also wish to purchase a booklet describing the use of programed texts in the classroom prepared by Behavioral Research Lab as an introduction to the subject. The complete program requires no teaching experience for group or individual work.

This is a programed series which assumes some knowledge of the alphabet and pre-reading letter and word discrimination skills. Words are taught primarily as pairs of words and phrases through discrimination of different short vowels and object pictures. Short sentences are then formed using pictures as prompts. As new words are learned, they are combined in various syntactical structures. For example, *can* is learned as an isolated noun and also as a verb. Later, long vowels, some inflected endings and a few initial consonant word elements are learned as discriminating elements.

Before continuing the workbook sequence, an accompanying reader accords more practice. Pupils alternate, reading first one programed text and then its correlated reader. Teacher-pupil interaction is encouraged by general questions the teacher may ask.

Program placement is accomplished through short tests which reproduce items contained in the programed sections. Thus, the tests have face validity. Test format facilitates ease of scoring and rapid placement in appropriate work. This provision for rapid program placement is considered by the examiners to be important in preventing too easy or too difficult beginning instruction and subsequent dropouts.

NO   1. materials have an adult appearance
NO   2. covers mark the owners as illiterates

NO   3. contents reflect adult tastes and interests

NO   4. contents reflect adult basic education need for acculturation and re-socialization

NO   5. presents problems of social maintenance as filling in forms, keeping accounts, making time purchases

NO   6. presents citizenship or civic responsibility content

NO   7. presents problems of social adjustment

NO   8. presents special information such as technical content suitable for specific trades or job descriptions

NO   9. suitable for English as a second literate language class

YES   10. placement test (s) included in materials

YES   11. placement test easily administered

YES   12. placement test quickly places individual into materials at appropriate level of difficulty

YES   13. materials programed

YES   14. includes practice reading materials

YES   15. practice readings are short

NO   16. practice reading includes comprehension questions

?   17. program difficult for adults (Note: May be difficult; reports of field testing needed.)

YES   18. sequentially organized skill building

NO   19. includes phonic skill training

YES   20. includes context skill training

YES   21. includes word analysis skills by word form

NO   22. includes dictionary skills

NO   23. includes other fact locating skills such as reading telephone directories

NO   24. includes map or graph reading training

NO   25. includes list of vocabulary introduced

NO   26. vocabulary taken from a standard frequency list such as the Lorge or Mitzel list

YES   28. includes teaching manual

YES   29. manual includes lesson plans

YES   30. manual includes teaching methods

YES   31. manual describes organization of material

YES 32. provides means for self-evaluation

YES 33. self-evaluation is frequent

YES 34. self-evaluation is part of learning program

NO 35. includes handwriting training and practice

NO 36. includes speech training and practice

YES 37. pupil works mainly by himself with minimum of teacher help

NO 38. group work supports the effort of individual

NO 39. materials have been field tested

NO 40. population upon which materials tested is described

NO 41. results of field testing are reported

NO 42. materials have been revised according to results of field testing

YES 43. illustrations augment instruction

NO 44. illustrations are tasteful

YES 45. illustrations are clearly and unambiguously related to text

YES 46. materials are durable

YES 47. materials are inexpensive

YES 48. materials are consumable (workbooks)

YES 49. style of type is pleasing

YES 50. layout design is pleasing

• _Collier-Macmillan International_
  (_also available from New Readers Press_)

• THE NEW STREAMLINED ENGLISH SERIES, 1966
  FRANK C. LAUBACH, ELIZABETH MOONEY KIRK,
  AND ROBERT S. LAUBACH

New Streamlined English is a programed series using the Laubach literacy system. Five workbooks provide training in the recognition of letter sounds, vowel sounds (long, short, 'other'), and sounds of some consonants. The sequence is similar to that in the _Streamlined English Series,_ revised edition. Writing practice is integrated into units, however, unlike that series. The teacher's manual was not available at the time this bibliography was published. Laubach Literacy, Inc. recommends a short literacy course for instructors. Therefore, the series probably should not be used by untrained teachers. As with all Laubach materials, type size appears inordinantly large. However, Laubach may have found this contributes to program success.

From examination of Skill Book 1, it would appear this is the most carefully designed and printed series from the aesthetic point of view. Materials have an adult appearance. They are like numerous other workbooks which adult students might use. The series would seem not to provide a placement test, however. This drawback might be remedied by several means that competent instructors might devise, including having the student read some of the practice passages to estimate level of competence. Perhaps this is suggested in the manual.

The series includes the following: Part 1: five skill books, five correlated readers, teacher's guide, and wall charts. Part 2: two readers containing practical writing practice and teacher's guide.

No Evaluation — not all materials on hand

• Croft Educational Services

• HOME AND FAMILY LIFE SERIES, 1949
EMMA LEWIS BRIGHT AND EVA CORNELIA MITCHELL

The series takes a whole word and sentence approach to reading. Special effort is made to be interracial in story content and illustrations. No specific time allotments are suggested.

Reading Placement is a short test of word recognition and sentence comprehension designed to provide the teacher with a brief indication of students' reading ability, which will be useful in grouping and in selecting appropriate reading materials.

Readers 1–4 — *A Day with the Brown Family, Making A*

Good Living, The Browns at School, and _The Browns and Their Neighbors_ — are divided into units dealing with the activities of the Brown family. The units are not subdivided into short stories, but each page is self-contained and is illustrated. Detailed lesson plans are given in _Three Instructional Tools for Teachers._ The emphasis is upon building a sight vocabulary and oral discussion of the subject matter.

Learning to Read Better, a workbook which accompanies the first reader, stresses the development of immediate recognition of words and phrases introduced in the reader and provides training in auditory and visual perception and comprehension skill development.

The _Language Workbook,_ designed to accompany the four readers, provides practice in writing, basic grammar, and oral expression. The reading that is done in connection with these exercises depends upon sight recognition of the words. The content focuses upon such practical skills as using the calendar and writing letters.

Three Instructional Tools for Teachers serves as a detailed teacher's guide for _Reading Placement, Learning to Read Better,_ and _Readers One, Two,_ and _Three._

YES	1.	materials have an adult appearance
NO	2.	covers mark the owners as illiterate
YES	3.	contents reflect adult tastes and interests
YES	4.	contents reflect adult basic education need for acculturation and re-socialization
YES	5.	presents problems of social maintenance as filling in forms, keeping accounts, making time purchases
YES	6.	presents citizenship or civic responsibility content
YES	7.	presents problems of social adjustment
NO	8.	present special information such as technical content suitable for specific trades or job descriptions
NO	9.	suitable for English as a second literate language class
YES	10.	placement test (s) included in materials

YES   11. placement test easily administered

YES   12. placement test quickly places individual into materials at appropriate level of difficulty

NO   13. materials programed

YES   14. includes practice reading materials

YES   15. practice readings are short

NO   16. practice reading includes comprehension questions

NO   17. program difficult for adults

YES   18. sequentially organized skill building

NO   19. includes phonic skill training

YES   20. includes context skill training

NO   21. includes word analysis skills by word form

NO   22. includes dictionary skills

NO   23. includes other fact locating skills such as reading telephone directories

NO   24. includes map or graph reading training

NO   25. includes list of vocabulary introduced

NO   26. vocabulary taken from a standard frequency list such as the Lorge or Mitzel list

YES   28. includes teaching manual

YES   29. manual includes lesson plans

YES   30. manual includes teaching methods

YES   31. manual describes organization of material

NO   32. provides means of self-evaluation

YES   35. includes handwriting training and practice

YES   36. includes speech training and practice

NO   37. pupil works mainly by himself with minimum of teacher help

YES   38. group work supports the efforts of individual

YES   39. materials have been field tested

YES   40. population upon which materials tested is described

NO   41. results of field testing are reported

YES   42. materials have been revised according to results of field testing

YES   43. illustrations augment instruction

NO   44. illustrations are tasteful

YES 45. illustrations are clearly and unambiguously related to text
YES 46. materials are durable
YES 47. materials are inexpensive
YES 48. materials are consumable
NO   49. style of type is pleasing
NO   50. layout design is pleasing

• *Encyclopedia Britannica Press*

• WORDS IN COLOR, 1962
  CALEB GATTEGNO

Words in Color is a preliminary reading program using 47 different colors to introduce the 47 different English sounds. The approach is basically phonic. Word patterns are introduced linguistically. Sounds are first learned in isolation in the usual pattern of short vowels with some consonants. These are combined into words, which are combined into short sentences. Irregular signs or sounds are then introduced.

Two manuals are provided for the teacher. One is devoted to the general approach, its origin and its psychological justification. The second contains teaching methods and lesson plans.

The sounds are introduced through a sequence of 21 colored wall charts. A second set of charts presents the vowel and consonant sounds and their variant spellings. Syntactical practice is provided by 1,356 different word cards, in which each part of speech is represented by a different colored card. Pupils combine the cards to form sentences.

Each pupil receives a series of three workbooks. Book 1 contains the short vowel sounds and four consonant sounds, which are combined into phrases and short sentences. Book 2 enlarges on this treatment, introducing all the regular vowel and consonant spellings with a greater number of practice words and sentences. Book 3 introduces the reading and writing of more unexpected graphemic representations the student has learned through the wall charts. Each successive chart elaborates upon the preceding chart through the addition of major symbol relationships and an increasing number of variants. After completing Books 1 and 2, students begin a soft cover book of stories for more practice. Fourteen work sheets in soft cover books follow class lessons, workbooks, and stories. Each sheet, to use the publishers' terms, "comprises several pages in the workbook and a variety of activities."

The program is devoted basically to teaching word analysis and syntax; practice in connected reading is limited. The program is not designed as a package to cover basic literacy. Teachers should plan to use other series to continue instruction.

NO 1. materials have an adult appearance
NO 2. covers mark the owners as illiterates
NO 3. contents reflect adult tastes and interests
NO 4. contents reflect adult basic education need for acculturation and re-socialization
NO 5. presents problems of social maintenance as filling in forms, keeping accounts, making time purchases
NO 6. present citizenship or civic responsibility content
NO 7. presents problems of social adjustment
NO 8. presents special information such as technical content suitable for specific trades of job descriptions
NO 9. suitable for English as a second literate language class
NO 10. placement test(s) included in materials
NO 13. materials programed
YES 14. includes practice reading materials
YES 15. practice readings are short
NO 16. practice reading includes comprehension questions
YES 17. program difficult for adults
YES 18. sequentially organized skill building
YES 19. includes phonic skill training
NO 20. includes context skill training

NO   21. includes word analysis skills by word form

NO   22. includes dictionary skills

NO   23. includes other fact locating skills such as reading telephone directories

NO   24. includes map or graph reading training

YES   25. includes list of vocabulary introduced

NO   26. vocabulary taken from a standard frequency list such as the Lorge or Mitzel list

YES   28. includes teaching manual

YES   29. manual includes lesson plans

YES   30. manual includes teaching methods

YES   31. manual describes organization of material

NO   32. provides means for self-evaluation

NO   35. includes handwriting training and practice

NO   36. includes speech training and practice

NO   37. pupil works mainly by himself with minimum of teacher help

YES   38. group work supports the effort of individual

YES   39. materials have been field tested

YES   40. population upon which materials tested is described

NO   41. results of field testing are reported

YES   42. materials have been revised according to results of field testing

NO   43. illustrations augment instruction

YES   46. materials are durable

YES   47. materials are inexpensive

NO   48. materials are consumable

YES   49. style of type is pleasing

YES   50. layout design is pleasing

• _Follett Publishing Company_

• COMMUNICATIONS, 1965
  DR. JOSEPHINE BAUER

Through the use of linguistic patterns the student is taught the letter sounds and words, primarily through writing. The materials are not programed, and no specific time allotments are made. Although materials were ordered through the usual commercial channels, delivery of the complete set was not made. Therefore, the evaluation is based upon *Getting Started: Communication I* only. The complete series includes: *Getting Started* (levels 0–2), *On the Way* (levels 3–4), and *Full Speed Ahead* (levels 5–6). There is teacher's manual, but instructions are printed on each page of the books.

Getting Started

Instruction begins with the alphabet. Students learn to produce upper case manuscript and upper and lower case cursive letters in the initial lessons. Then they are introduced to the roman alphabet used in printed materials and to short, regular words. Most of the words have but one syllable, with a "short vowel" and the most common consonant sounds. Phonic skills, primarily the analysis of phoneme groups, are introduced with a linguistic rationale. Much writing practice, rather than extensive reading of passages or stories, is used to reinforce learnings.

NO   1. materials have an adult appearance

NO   2. covers mark the owners as illiterates

NO   3. contents reflect adult tastes and interests

YES 4. contents reflect adult basic education need for acculturation and re-socialization

NO   5. presents problems of social maintenance as filling in forms, keeping accounts, making time purchases

NO   6. presents citizenship or civic responsibility content

NO   7. presents problems of social adjustment

NO   8. presents special information such as technical content suitable for specific trades of job descriptions

NO   9. suitable for English as a second literate language class

NO 10. placement test (s) included in materials

NO 13. materials programed

YES 14. includes practice reading materials

YES 15. practice readings are short

NO 16. practice reading includes comprehension questions
NO 17. program difficult for adults
YES 18. sequentially organized skill building
YES 19. includes phonic skill training
YES 20. includes context skill training
YES 21. includes word analysis skills by word form
NO 22. includes dictionary skills
NO 23. includes other fact locating skills such as reading telephone directories
NO 24. includes map or graph reading training
NO 25. includes list of vocabulary introduced
NO 26. vocabulary taken from a standard list such as the Lorge or Mitzel list
NO 28. includes teaching manual
NO 32. provides means for self-evaluation
YES 35. includes handwriting training and practice
NO 36. includes speech training and practice
NO 37. pupil works mainly by himself with minimum of teacher help
YES 38. group work supports the effort of individual
NO 39. materials have been field tested
YES 43. illustrations augment instruction
NO 44. illustrations are tasteful
YES 45. illustrations are clearly and unambiguously related to text
YES 46. materials are durable
YES 47. materials are inexpensive
YES 48. materials are consumable
YES 49. style of type is pleasing
YES 50. layout design is pleasing

• READING FOR A PURPOSE, 1965
J. B. ADAIR AND R. L. CURRY

Reading for a Purpose is a one-volume language arts program for classroom use. The integrated lessons include reading, handwriting, and English usage. Instruction is initially through the whole word approach. Later lessons include inflected endings and initial consonants, including blends. A single basic format is used for each reading lesson. The teacher introduces a large number of new words taken from the accompanying story by writing them in isolation on the chalkboard. The story is then read. Since many new words are introduced, often more than 20, and since all reading selections are short, usually less than half a page, the number of times a new word is met in context is extremely small. In part this is rectified by exercises, some of which also introduce content and writing skills. Handwriting practice is also limited to following some models presented by the text. Pupils probably will require more letter formation practice than is provided, unless they have had some previous handwriting instruction. Lessons are provided in map reading and dictionary use. However, neither subject is covered in the depth sixth-grade proficiency, the level claimed by the publisher, would seem to require.

The rapid introduction of words and skills and the paucity of practice materials makes the use of correlated materials from other sources mandatory. No provision is made for entry into the program other than at the beginning. Neither is there provision for the pupil to assess his own progress. Assessment of pupil progress will require construction of correlated exercises or use of a standardized test.

The story content of the lessons is appropriate to an adult audience. Social skills necessary for developing coping behaviors are treated, though not in depth and not extensively. For example, budgeting and good health are each the subject of one lesson consisting of a few paragraphs; yet budgeting is a chronic problem among the socially disadvantaged, while poor health and poor health habits are endemic.

YES   1. materials have an adult appearance

NO   2. covers mark the owners as illiterates

YES   3. contents reflect adult tastes and interests

YES   4. contents reflect adult basic education need for acculturation and re-socialization

YES   5. presents problems of social maintenance as filling in forms, keeping accounts, making time purchases

NO   6. presents citizenship or civic responsibility content

NO   7. presents problems of social adjustment

NO   8. presents special information such as technical content suitable for specific trades or job descriptions

NO   9. suitable for English as a second literate language class

NO   10. placement test (s) included in materials

NO   13. materials programed

YES 14. includes practice reading materials

YES 15. practice readings are short

NO   16. practice reading includes comprehension questions

NO   17. program difficult for adults

YES 18. sequentially organized skill building

YES 19. includes phonic skill training

YES 20. includes context skill training

YES 21. includes word analysis skills by word form

YES 22. includes dictionary skills

YES 23. includes other fact locating skills such as reading telephone directories

NO   24. includes map or graph reading training

NO   25. includes list of vocabulary introduced

NO   26. vocabulary taken from a standard frequency list such as the Lorge or Mitzel list

YES 28. includes teaching manual

YES 29. manual includes lesson plans

NO   30. manual includes teaching methods

YES 31. manual describes organization of material

YES 32. provides means for self-evaluation

NO   33. self-evaluation is frequent

NO   34. self-evaluation is part of learning program

YES   35. includes handwriting training and practice

YES   36. includes speech training and practice

NO   37. pupil works mainly by himself with minimum of teacher help

YES   38. group work supports the effort of individual

NO   39. materials have been field tested

YES   43. illustrations augment instruction

YES   44. illustrations are tasteful

YES   45. illustrations are clearly and unambiguously related to text

YES   46. materials are durable

NO   47. materials are inexpensive

YES   48. materials are consumable

YES   49. style of type is pleasing

YES   50. layout is pleasing

· SYSTEM FOR SUCCESS, BOOK 1, 1965
R. LEE HENNEY

This program covers the areas of reading, writing, spelling, arithmetic, and English usage. The goal is fourth-grade level of proficiency in these skills. Both phonic and linguistic methods are employed for reading instruction. Phonics lessons, the first step of instruction, take the form of drill charts. Letter sounds are learned first, then blends at the beginnings of words; and finally word families are learned by the substitution of different initial elements. Practice in sentence reading does not begin until the student has developed a considerable repertoire of words and word attack skills through use of the charts. Arithmetic lessons are in a separate section. These lessons combine reading problems with calculation practice, up to and including multiplication and division of whole numbers. The English usage section contains practice for competency in those skills necessary for letter writing, such as abbreviations, capitalization, punctuation and letter form, as well as recognition of appropriate verb forms and tenses. Lessons on sentence structure contain grammatical terminology not usually found in basic literacy programs.

Content of the reading practice selections is keyed to the tasks of young adults. *System for Success, Book 1,* is suitable for small groups, and it is a program which requires competent instruction. It may have to be supplemented by additional, correlated reading practice.

YES	1.	materials have an adult appearance
NO	2.	covers mark the owners as illiterates
YES	3.	contents reflect adult tastes and interests
YES	4.	contents reflect adult basic education need for acculturation and re-socialization
YES	5.	presents problems of social maintenance as filling in forms, keeping accounts, making time purchases
NO	6.	presents citizenship or civic responsibility content
NO	7.	presents problems of social adjustment
NO	8.	present special information such as technical content suitable for specific trades or job descriptions
NO	9.	suitable for English as a second literate language class
NO	10.	placement test(s) included in materials
NO	13.	materials programed
YES	14.	includes practice reading materials
YES	15.	practice readings are short
YES	16.	practice reading includes comprehension questions
YES	17.	program difficult for adults
YES	18.	sequentially organized skill building
YES	19.	includes phonic skill training
NO	20.	includes context skill training
YES	21.	includes word analysis skills by word form
NO	22.	includes dictionary skills
NO	23.	includes other fact locating skills such as reading telephone directories
NO	24.	includes map or graph reading training
NO	25.	includes list of vocabulary introduced

NO 26. vocabulary taken from a standard frequency list such as the Lorge or Mitzel List

YES 28. includes teaching manual

YES 29. manual includes lesson plans

YES 30. manual includes teaching methods

YES 31. manual describes organization of material

NO 32. provides means for self-evaluation

YES 35. includes handwriting training and practice

NO 36. includes speech training and practice

NO 37. pupil works mainly by himself with minimum of teacher help

NO 38. group work supports the effort of individual

YES 39. materials have been field tested

YES 40. population upon which materials tested is described

NO 41. results of field testing are reported

YES 42. materials have been revised according to results of field testing

NO 43. illustrations augment instruction

YES 46. materials are durable

YES 47. materials are inexpensive

YES 48. materials are consumable

YES 49. style of type is pleasing

NO 50. layout design is pleasing

· *Government Printing Office*

· MEN IN THE ARMED FORCES MB 001, 1956,
SERVICEMEN LEARN TO READ MB 001.2
LOWRY W. HARDING AND JAMES B. BURR

The reader, *Men in the Armed Forces,* and its accompanying, correlated workbook, *Servicemen Learn to Read,* utilize the whole work method of instruction and are specifically designed for the armed forces. Structural analysis is also introduced as a word attack skill. The reader contains stories particularly pertinent to military life. A sight vocabulary is built through simple sentences and workbook exercises. A set of large drill cards is used to present all new words. The cards contain sentence fragments and phrases. The workbook directions for instructors and the types of exercises are explicit enough for untrained teachers. Both the reader and the workbook include a considerable amount of coordinated practice materials. Cursive writing charts in the workbook are not elaborated upon, so non-writers will probably require supplementary practice. These books have soft covers, but they are substantially constructed.

YES	1.	materials have an adult appearance
YES	2.	covers mark the owners as illiterates
YES	3.	contents reflect adult tastes and interests
NO	4.	contents reflect adult basic education need for acculturation and re-socialization
NO	5.	presents problems of social maintenance as filling in forms, keeping accounts, making time purchases
YES	6.	present citizenship or civic responsibility content
NO	7.	presents problems of social adjustment
YES	8.	presents special information such as technical content suitable for specific trades or job descriptions
NO	9.	suitable for English as a second literate language class
NO	10.	placement test(s) included in materials
NO	13.	materials programed
YES	14.	includes practice reading materials
YES	15.	practice readings are short
YES	16.	practice reading includes comprehension questions
NO	17.	program difficult for adults
YES	18.	sequentially organized skill building
NO	19.	includes phonic skill training
YES	20.	includes context skill training
YES	21.	includes word analysis skills by word form
NO	22.	includes dictionary skills
NO	23.	includes other fact locating skills such as reading telephone directories

NO   24. includes map or graph reading training

NO   25. includes list of vocabulary introduced

NO   26. vocabulary taken from a standard frequency list such as the Lorge of Mitzel list

YES 28. includes teaching manual

YES 29. manual includes lesson plans

NO   30. manual includes teaching methods

YES 31. manual describes organization of material

NO   32. provides means for self-evaluation

NO   35. includes handwriting training and practice

NO   36. includes speech training and practice

NO   37. pupil works mainly by himself with minimum of teacher help

YES 38. group work supports the efforts of individual

YES 39. materials have been field tested

YES 40. population upon which materials tested is described

NO   41. results of field testing are reported

YES 42. materials have been revised according to results of field testing

NO   43. illustrations augment instruction

NO   44. illustrations are tasteful

NO   45. illustrations are clearly and unambiguously related to text

YES 46. materials are durable

YES 47. materials are inexpensive

YES 48. materials are consumable: workbook

YES 49. style of type is pleasing

YES 50. layout design is pleasing

• *Harcourt, Brace, and World, Inc.*

• ENGLISH LESSONS FOR ADULTS, 1966
  JEWEL VARNADO AND PHILIP J. GEARING

The series begins with a whole word approach, but phonics and structural analysis skills are soon introduced. Very brief notes to the teacher are provided at the back of the books. No time allotments are made. Because Books 2 and 3 were not available at the time of publication, the evaluation is based on the first book only.

Book 1

After learning to print, the student practices printing a few sight words that are learned in association with pictures. He learns to spell the words through repetition, by copying them and by supplying missing letters. After studying the distinction between vowels and consonants, he learns the letter sounds by associating the names of drawings of sample objects with their beginning letter-sounds. He is introduced to phonics by studying letter-sounds in different positions in the words in his sight vocabulary. Some structural analysis skills are included later in the sequence.

YES   1. materials have an adult appearance

NO   2. covers mark the owners as illiterates

YES   3. contents reflect adult tastes and interests

NO   4. contents reflect adult basic education need for acculturation and re-socialization

NO   5. presents problems of social maintenance as filling forms, keeping accounts, making time purchases

NO   6. presents citizenship or civic responsibility content

NO   7. presents problems of social adjustment

NO   8. presents special information such as technical content suitable for specific trades or descriptions

YES   9. suitable for English as a second literate language class

NO   10. placement test(s) included in materials

NO   13. materials programed

YES   14. includes practice reading materials

YES   15. practice readings are short

NO   16. practice reading includes comprehension questions

YES   17. program difficult for adults

YES   18. sequentially organized skill building

YES   19. includes phonic skill training

NO   20. includes context skill training

YES   21. includes word analysis skills by word form

NO   22. includes dictionary skills

NO   23. includes other fact locating skills such as reading telephone directories

NO   24. includes map or graph reading training

YES   25. includes list of vocabulary introduced

NO   26. vocabulary taken from a standard frequency list such as the Lorge or Mitzel list

YES   28. includes teaching manual (Note: Very brief directions to the teacher are given at the end of the book.)

YES   29. manual includes lesson plans

NO   30. manual includes teaching methods

NO   31. manual describes organization of materials

YES   32. provides means for self-evaluation

YES   33. self-evaluation is frequent

YES   34. self-evaluation is part of learning program

YES   35. includes handwriting training and practice

NO   36. includes speech training and practice

NO   37. pupil works mainly by himself with minimum of teacher help

YES   38. group work supports the effort of individual

NO   39. materials have been field tested

YES   43. illustrations augment instruction

YES   44. illustrations are tasteful

YES   45. illustrations are clearly and unambiguously related to text (Note: A few illustrations are not directly related.)

YES   46. materials are durable

YES   47. materials are inexpensive

YES   48. materials are consumable

YES   49. style of type is pleasing

YES   50. layout design is pleasing

• *Holt, Rinehart and Winston, Inc.*

• ADULT BASIC EDUCATION: FIRST SERIES
ELLEN C. HENDERSON AND TWILA L. HENDERSON

Both reading and writing instruction are included in the two unprogramed, soft cover books. The method of teaching reading is linguistic and phonic, emphasizing spelling as an integral part of learning to read and write. No time limits for completion of the materials are specified.

Learning to Read and Write, 1965

From the beginning the authors stress proper eye movements and "inner speech." The first is established by encouraging the student to dwell no longer than necessary on a word and by teaching phrase reading early in the sequence. "Inner speech" involves the rapid recognition of unknown words by the consonant framework; but stress is always placed upon getting the meaning directly from known words without pronouncing them.

At the beginning stage words are taught as wholes, mainly by association with pictures, to establish word meaning relationships; the alphabet is taught; and proper eye movement habits are established. The basis for recognizing new words is generally through the consonant sounds. Rules for sounding consonants are taught deductively. Then the students are given skeleton words, with the vowels omitted, for recognition practice.

The book also includes some work on structural analysis and correct pronunciation. Printing is taught at the beginning of the book, but cursive writing is stressed throughout. At the end of the book extended reading selections about one family are presented. Although no comprehension exercises are included, there is some work in word study. A teacher's guide is provided at the end of the book.

Learning to Write, 1965

This workbook is described by the authors as a complete handwriting instruction and practice book. The first section of the book deals with manuscript writing. The letters are grouped according to shape and students are encouraged to practice until making the letter forms has become automatic. Then the transition to cursive writing, to which the second section of the book is devoted, is made.

YES   1. materials have an adult appearance
YES   2. covers mark the owners as illiterates
YES   3. contents reflect adult tastes and interests
NO   4. contents reflect adult basic education need for acculturation and re-socialization
NO   5. presents problems of social maintenance as filling in forms, keeping accounts, making time purchases
NO   6. presents citizenship or civic responsibility content
NO   7. presents problems of social adjustment
NO   8. presents special information such as technical content suitable for specific trades or job descriptions
NO   9. suitable for English as a second literate language class
NO   10. placement test(s) included in materials
NO   13. materials programed
YES   14. includes practice reading materials
YES   15. practice readings are short
NO   16. practice reading includes comprehension questions
YES   17. program difficult for adults
YES   18. sequentially organized skill building
YES   19. includes phonic skill training
NO   20. includes context skill training
YES   21. includes word analysis skills by word form
YES   22. includes dictionary skills
NO   23. includes other fact locating skills such as reading telephone directories
NO   24. includes map or graph reading training
YES   25. includes list of vocabulary introduced

NO   26. vocabulary taken from a standard frequency list such as the Lorge or Mitzel List
YES 28. includes teaching manual
YES 29. manual includes lesson plans
YES 30. manual includes teaching methods
YES 31. manual describes organization of material
NO   32. provides means for self-evaluation
YES 35. includes handwriting training and practice
NO   36. includes speech training and practice
NO   37. pupil works mainly by himself with minimum of teacher help
NO   38. group work supports the effort of individual
NO   39. materials have been field tested
YES 43. illustrations augment instruction
YES 44. illustrations are tasteful
YES 45. illustrations are clearly and unambiguously related to text
YES 46. materials are durable
YES 47. materials are inexpensive
NO   48. materials are consumable
YES 49. style of type is pleasing
YES 50. layout design is pleasing

• ELEMENTARY EDUCATION FOR ADULTS, 1950
  ALBERT A. OWENS AND WILLIAM SHARLIP

The book, *Elementary Education for Adults,* is dated by the pictures. No time allotments are made, nor is a teacher's guide included. The approach is primarily through the whole sentence.

The student first associates short sentences with pictures and then studies the individual words in the exercises. Handwriting is also taught early in the book. After a basic vocabulary has been established, work is given in spelling, recognition of signs, and phonics. In the last section of the book, stories of progressively greater length are introduced. Practice is also given in writing letters.

YES 1. materials have an adult appearance

YES 2. covers mark the owners as illiterates

YES 3. contents reflect adult tastes and interests

YES 4. contents reflect adult basic education need for acculturation and re-socialization

YES 5. presents problems of social maintenance as filling in forms, keeping accounts, making time purchases

NO 6. presents citizenship or civic responsibility content

NO 7. presents problems of social adjustment

NO 8. presents special information such as technical content suitable for specific trades of job descriptions

NO 9. suitable for English as a second literate language class

NO 10. placement test(s)

NO 13. materials programed

YES 14. includes practice reading materials

YES 15. practice readings are short

NO 16. practice reading includes comprehension questions

NO 17. program difficult for adults

YES 18. sequentially organized skill building

YES 19. includes phonic skill training

NO 20. includes context skill training

NO 21. includes word analysis skills by word form

NO 22. includes dictionary skills

NO 23. includes other fact locating skills such as reading telephone directories

NO 24. includes map or graph reading training

NO 25. includes list of vocabulary introduced

NO 26. vocabulary taken from a standard frequency list such as the Lorge or Mitzel list

NO 28. includes teaching manual

NO 32. provides means for self-evaluation

YES 35. includes handwriting training and practice

NO 36. includes speech training and practice

NO 37. pupil works mainly by himself with minimum of teacher help

NO 38. group work supports the effort of individual

NO   39. materials have been field tested
YES   43. illustrations augment instruction
NO   44. illustrations are tasteful
NO   45. illustrations are clearly and unambiguously related to text
YES   46. materials are durable
YES   47. materials are inexpensive
YES   48. materials are consumable
YES   49. style of type is pleasing
NO   50. layout design is pleasing

> • *The Literacy Center*
> *Baylor Book Store*

• READING THE EASY TV-WAY, 1960
  SALLIE E. COOK AND LUCILLE E. BAYER

Reading the Easy TV-Way is a television adaptation of the Laubach approach to reading instruction. The Laubach method utilizes the similarity between familiar objects and letter shapes.

Pupils learn the sounds of the common consonants as they appear at the beginnings of words. For example, C is learned as C in *cup* (a heavy C is drawn as the outline of the picture of a cup). These words are then used in simple sentences and, finally, the words are combined in different ways for sentence variety. Letters are printed and the sentences learned are then copied.

This series provides only the preliminary instruction for a literacy program. The vocabulary introduced is quite restrictive. However, the three pamphlets might be used by a literate to encourage a non-literate to undertake a more complete literacy program. *Reading the Easy TV-Way* and *Writing the Easy Way*, a companion volume, are consumable. A trained teacher is not required.

YES   1. materials have an adult appearance
NO   2. covers mark the owners as illiterates

NO   3. contents reflect adult tastes and interests

NO   4. contents reflect adult basic education need for acculturation and re-socialization

NO   5. presents problems of social maintenance as filling in forms, keeping accounts, making time purchases

NO   6. presents citizenship or civic responsibility content

NO   7. presents problems of social adjustment

NO   8. presents special information such as technical content suitable for specific trades or job descriptions

NO   9. suitable for English as a second literate language class

NO   10. placement test(s) included in materials

NO   13. materials programed

YES 14. includes practice reading materials

YES 15. practice readings are short

NO   16. practice reading includes comprehension questions

NO   17. program difficult for adults

YES 18. sequentially organized skill building

YES 19. includes phonic skill training

NO   20. includes context skill training

NO   21. includes word analysis skills by word form

NO   22. includes dictionary skills

NO   23. includes other fact locating skills such as reading telephone directories

NO   24. includes map or graph reading training

NO   25. includes list of vocabulary introduced

NO   26. vocabulary taken from a standard frequency list such as the Lorge or Mitzel list

YES 28. includes teaching manual

YES 29. manual includes lesson plans

NO   30. manual includes teaching methods

NO   31. manual describes organization of material

NO   32. provides means for self-evaluation

NO   35. includes handwriting training and practice

NO   36. includes speech training and practice

NO   37. pupil works mainly by himself with minimum of teacher help

NO   38. group work supports the effort of individual

YES 39. materials have been field tested

NO   40. population upon with materials tested is described

NO   41. results of field testing are reported

NO   42. materials have been revised according to results of field testing

YES 43. illustrations augment instruction

YES 44. illustrations are tasteful

YES 45. illustrations are clearly and unambiguously related to text

YES 46. materials are durable

YES 47. materials are inexpensive

YES 48. materials are consumable

YES 49. style of type is pleasing

YES 50. layout design is pleasing

· *McGraw-Hill Book Company*

· PROGRAMED READING FOR ADULTS, 1966
  SULLIVAN ASSOCIATES

The series includes five programed workbooks and teacher's manuals. The beginning pupil is assumed to have certain skills, such as ability to print letters of the alphabet. Pairs of words with similar elements are introduced for purposes of teaching word discrimination and the differentiation of short vowels. Pictures are used as word prompts. Pupils must, therefore, see the relationship between the object pictured and the word. Experiential and language limitations of adult beginning readers may make it desirable for the teacher to pay closer attention to pupil responses than the programed format would seem to indicate, particularly with the first book in the program. Dialect differences may require supplementary practice; and the word-ideas contained in certain pictures may require explanation, even though they generally appear to be clear and unambiguous. New words are learned as they are combined in a variety of common syntactical patterns. The workbook titles — Book 1, *The Letters of the Alphabet;* Book 2, *The Sounds of the Letters;* Book 3, *From Words to Sentences;* Book 4, *Sentence Reading;* and Book 5, *Paragraph Reading* — should not be taken as indicative of the development of discrete reading skills. The introduction of new words and phrases occurs in Books 2 through 5; some sentences are learned in Book 2.

No placement test is provided. Less experienced teachers may find it difficult to use the program with socially deprived pupils. The program is suitable for tutorial or group instruction; although the material is programmed, a teacher is required.

YES	1.	materials have an adult appearance
NO	2.	covers mark the owners as illiterates
NO	3.	contents reflect adult tastes and interests
NO	4.	contents reflect adult basic education need for acculturation and re-socialization
NO	5.	presents problems of social maintenance as filling in forms, keeping accounts, making time purchases
NO	6.	presents citizenship or civic responsibility content
NO	7.	presents problems of social adjustment
NO	8.	presents special information such as technical content suitable for specific trades or job descriptions
NO	9.	suitable for English as a second literate language class
NO	10.	placement test(s) included in materials
YES	13.	materials programed
NO	14.	includes practice reading materials
YES	17.	program difficult for adults
YES	18.	sequentially organized skill building
YES	19.	includes phonic skill training
YES	20.	includes context skill training
YES	21.	includes word analysis skills by word form
NO	22.	includes dictionary skills
NO	23.	includes other fact locating skills such as reading telephone directories

NO   24. includes map or graph reading training
NO   25. includes list of vocabulary introduced
NO   26. vocabulary taken from a standard frequency list such as the Lorge or Mitzel list
YES 28. includes teaching manual
YES 29. manual includes lesson plans
NO   31. manual describes organization of material
YES 32. provides means for self-evaluation
YES 33. self-evaluation is frequent
YES 34. self-evaluation is part of learning program
NO   35. includes handwriting training and practice
YES 36. includes speech training and practice
YES 37. pupil works mainly by himself with minimum of teacher help
NO   38. group work supports the effort of individual
NO   39. materials have been field tested
YES 43. illustrations augment instruction
NO   45. illustrations are clearly and unambiguously related to text
YES 46. materials are durable
YES 47. materials are inexpensive
YES 48. materials are consumable
NO   49. style of type is pleasing
YES 50. layout is pleasing

> • *National Association of Public
> School Adult Educators*

• OPERATION ALPHABET, 1962
  TV HOME STUDY BOOK

Operation Alphabet is a whole word method workbook intended for use with the School District of Philadelphia home television series, which was developed to promote adult literacy. The series was designed to encourage adults to enroll in literacy programs, but the workbook has been used as a self-contained unit.

The book contains 100 one-page lessons. Manuscript letter forms are taught in both upper and lower case, and printing practice is part of each lesson. Goals are modest: ". . . he will be able to recognize, understand and use more words. He will be able to read some signs and directions, and he will be able to write better."

YES	1.	materials have an adult appearance
NO	2.	covers mark the owners as illiterates
YES	3.	contents reflect adult tastes and interests
NO	4.	contents reflect adult basic education need for acculturation and re-socialization
NO	5.	presents problems of social maintenance as filling in forms, keeping accounts, making time purchases
NO	6.	presents citizenship or civic responsibility content
NO	7.	presents problems of social adjustment
NO	8.	presents special information such as technical content suitable for specific trades of job descriptions
NO	9.	suitable for English as a second literate language class
NO	10.	placement test(s) included in materials
NO	13.	materials programed
YES	14.	includes practice reading materials
YES	15.	practice readings are short
YES	16.	practice reading includes comprehension questions
NO	17.	program difficult for adults
NO	18.	sequentially organized skill training
NO	20.	includes context skill training
NO	21.	includes word analysis skills by word form
NO	22.	includes dictionary skills
NO	23.	includes other fact locating skills such as reading telephone directories
NO	24.	includes map or graph reading training
NO	25.	includes list of vocabulary introduced
NO	26.	vocabulary taken from a standard frequency list such as the Lorge or Mitzel list
NO	28.	includes teaching manual

NO   32. provides means for self-evaluation
NO   35. includes handwriting training and practice
NO   37. pupil works mainly by himself with minimum of
      teacher help
NO   38. group work supports the effort of individual
YES   39. materials have been field tested
NO   40. population upon which materials tested is described
NO   41. results of field testing are reported
NO   42. materials have been revised according to results of
      field testing
YES   43. illustrations augment instruction
YES   44. illustrations are tasteful
YES   45. illustrations are clearly and unambiguously related
      to text
YES   46. materials are durable
YES   47. materials are inexpensive
YES   48. materials are consumable
YES   49. style of type is pleasing
YES   50. layout design is pleasing

• *New Readers Press (also Macmillan Co.)*

• THE STREAMLINED ENGLISH SERIES, REVISED EDITION, 1955
FRANK C. LAUBACH

This is a non-programed series for class instruction by competent literacy instructors using the Laubach system. The Laubach literacy system utilizes the similarity between objects and
letter forms. Pupils first learn to identify and to write letters
through charts and a writing workbook. Lessons cover the
more common spellings of the most useful sounds or sound
groups, or the more common sounds associated with frequently
encountered spellings. Upon successful completion of *Streamlined English* pupils have a vocabulary of approximately 1,100
words. Continued growth is provided by a reader, short,
paperbacked supplementary readers, and a two-level weekly
newspaper.

YES   1. materials have an adult appearance

YES   2. covers do not mark the owners as illiterates

YES   3. contents reflect adult tastes and interests

NO   4. contents reflect adult basic education need for acculturation and re-socialization

NO   5. presents problems of social maintenance as filling in forms, keeping accounts, making time purchases

NO   6. presents citizenship or civic responsibility content

NO   7. presents problems of social adjustment

NO   8. presents special information such as technical content suitable for specific trades or job descriptions

NO   9. suitable for English as a second literate language class

NO   10. placement test(s) included in materials

YES   13. materials programed

YES   14. includes practice reading materials

YES   15. practice readings are short

YES   16. practice reading includes comprehension questions

NO   17. program difficult for adults

YES   18. sequentially organized skill building

YES   19. includes phonic skill training

NO   20. includes context skill training

NO   21. includes word analysis skills by word form

NO   22. includes dictionary skills

NO   23. includes other fact locating skills such as reading telephone directories

NO   24. includes map or graph reading training

YES   25. includes list of vocabulary introduced

NO   26. vocabulary taken from a standard frequency list such as the Lorge or Mitzel list

YES   28. includes teaching manual

YES   29. manual includes lesson plans

YES   30. manual includes teaching methods

NO   31. manual describes organization of material

YES   32. provides means for self-evaluation

YES   33. self-evaluation is frequent

YES   34. self-evaluation is part of learning program

YES 35. includes handwriting training and practice

NO 36. includes speech training and practice

NO 37. pupil works mainly by himself with minimum of teacher help

YES 38. group work supports the effort of individual

YES 39. materials have been field tested

NO 40. population upon which materials tested is described

NO 41. results of field testing are reported

YES 42. materials have been revised according to results of field testing

YES 43. illustrations augment instruction

NO 44. illustrations are tasteful

YES 45. illustrations are clearly and unambiguously related to text

YES 46. materials are durable

YES 47. materials are inexpensive

YES 48. materials are consumable

YES 49. style of type is pleasing

NO 50. layout design is pleasing

· *Noble and Noble Publishers, Inc.*

· ADULT BASIC EDUCATION SERIES, 1966

The approach to reading instruction is through the use of whole words and sentences. The material is not programed and no specific time is recommended for completion of the sequence. The 1966 revisions are in soft covers.

From Words to Stories, 1966
Mary L. Guyton and Margaret E. Kielty

The purpose of this book is to build a basic sight vocabulary by introducing new words and providing for repetition of known words in short, unrelated stories and review exercises. The book contains a "Suggestions for the Teacher" section which includes suggested techniques and instructional patterns for the lessons.

How We Live, 1966
Angelica W. Cass

This book may be used for beginning instruction. There is no apparent correlation with *From Words to Stories,* except that the approach is still through whole words and sentences. Initial sight words are introduced as labels for pictures. The rest of the book comprises short stories, word lists, comprehension and vocabulary usage exercises, and suggestions for writing practice. Much of the instructional task is left to the inventiveness of the teacher.

Your Family and Your Job, 1966

The book builds upon skills developed in *How We Live* and is designed to take the adult student beyond the beginning stage. Reading selections make use of an expanded vocabulary to make usage more natural. Exercises following the selections provide comprehension checks, instruction in grammar and usage and occasion for written work. Emphasis is placed upon written rather than oral responses.

YES 1. materials have an adult appearance

NO 2. covers do not mark the owners as illiterates

YES 3. contents reflect adult tastes and interests

YES 4. contents reflect adult basic education need for acculturation and re-socialization

YES 5. presents problems of social maintenance as filling in forms, keeping accounts, making time purchases

NO 6. presents citizenship or civic responsibility content

YES 7. presents problems of social adjustment

NO 8. presents special information such as technical content suitable for specific trades of job descriptions

NO 9. suitable for English as a second literate language class

NO 10. placement test(s) included in materials

NO 13. materials programed

YES 14. includes practice reading materials

YES 15. practice readings are short

YES 16. practice reading includes comprehension questions

NO 17. program difficult for adults

NO 18. sequentially organized skill building

NO 19. includes phonic skill training

NO 20. includes context skill training

YES 21. includes word analysis skills by word form

NO 22. includes dictionary skills

NO 23. includes other fact locating skills such as reading telephone directories

NO 24. includes map or graph reading training

NO 25. includes list of vocabulary introduced

NO 26. vocabulary taken from a standard frequency list such as the Lorge or Mitzel list

NO 28. includes teaching manual

NO 29. manual includes lesson plans

YES 30. manual includes teaching methods

NO 31. manual describes organization of material

NO 32. provides means for self-evaluation

NO 35. includes handwriting training and practice

NO 36. includes speech training and practice

NO 37. pupil works mainly by himself with minimum of teacher help

YES 38. group work supports the effort of individual

YES 39. materials have been field tested

NO 40. population upon which materials tested is described

NO 41. results of field testing are reported

YES 42. materials have been revised according to results of field testing

YES 43. illustrations augment instruction

YES 44. illustrations are tasteful

NO 45. illustrations are clearly and unambiguously related to text

YES 46. materials are durable

YES 47. materials are inexpensive

NO 48. materials are consumable

YES 49. style of type is pleasing
YES 50. layout design is pleasing

• *Science Research Associates, Inc.*

• READING IN HIGH GEAR, CYCLE I, 1964
MYRON WOOLMAN

Cycle I is a part of a three section (cycle) series, which the publishers say will lead to eighth-grade reading proficiency when successfully completed. Cycle I includes two teacher's manuals and four consumable workbooks. The materials are partly programed and partly tutorial; the teacher reads prepared statements and supervises practice. Instruction begins at the readiness level. Letters are learned gradually and combined into short words, inflections, and sentences. The sequence is, roughly, from most commonly to least commonly encountered sounds. Discriminating letters and discovering relationships between picture clues and words are important elements of instruction. Printing is taught. Short reading selections and puzzles provide for reading and printing practice.

YES 1. materials have an adult appearance
YES 2. covers do not mark the owners as illiterates
NO   3. contents reflect adult tastes and interests
NO   4. contents reflect adult basic education need for acculturation and re-socialization
NO   5. presents problems of social maintenance as filling in forms, keeping accounts, making time purchases
NO   6. presents citizenship or civic responsibility content
NO   7. presents problems of social adjustment
NO   8. presents special information such as technical content suitable for specific trades or job descriptions
NO   9. suitable for English as a second literate language class
NO   10. placement test(s) included in materials
YES 13. materials programed

YES 14. includes practice reading materials
YES 15. practice readings are short
NO   16. practice reading includes comprehension questions
NO   17. program difficult for adults
YES 18. sequentially organized skill building
YES 19. includes phonic skill training
YES 20. includes context skill training
NO   21. includes word analysis skills by word form
NO   22. includes dictionary skills
NO   23. includes other fact locating skills such as reading telephone directories
NO   24. includes map or graph reading training
NO   25. includes list of vocabulary introduced
NO   26. vocabulary taken from a standard frequency list such as the Lorge or Mitzel list
YES 28. includes teaching manual
YES 29. manual includes lesson plans
YES 30. manual includes teaching methods
YES 31. manual describes organization of material
YES 32. provides means for self-evaluation
YES 33. self-evaluation is frequent
YES 34. self-evaluation is part of learning program
YES 35. includes handwriting training and practice
NO   36. includes speech training and practice
YES 37. pupil works mainly by himself with minimum of teacher help
NO   38. group work supports the effort of individual
NO   39. materials have been field tested
NO   40. population upon which materials tested is described
NO   41. results of field testing are reported
NO   42. materials have been revised according to results of field testing
YES 43. illustrations augment instruction
NO   44. illustrations are tasteful
YES 45. illustrations are clearly and unambiguously related to text

YES   46. materials are durable
NO   47. materials are inexpensive
YES   48. materials are consumable
NO   49. style of type is pleasing
YES   50. layout design is pleasing

· *Silver Burdett Company*

· BASIC READING SERIES

The *Basic Reading Series* is in the process of being published. The series is organized on four levels to provide for individual differences in ability. Level one will include six consumable text-workbooks and a *Teacher's Edition.* Supplementary materials will include flash cards, recordings, and projectuals. The intent is to bring the adult up to sixth-grade reading ability.

· BUILDING YOUR LANGUAGE POWER
FRANK C. LAUBACH
PROGRAMED BY WILLIAM C. WOLF, JR.

These programed materials are linguistic in approach and based mainly on visual and phonic discrimination of letters. An untrained reading teacher may administer the program because each student works mainly by himself. No specific time limits are set for the completion of the program.

Books 1–6

The program comprises six books with markers that reveal only a portion of a page at a time. By the end of the last book the successful student is able to read about 1,300 basic English words at sight and to attack new words as well.

Printing is taught by superimposing a letter shape over a picture of a familiar object beginning with that letter. Gradually the picture and the letter shape are dissociated, and the student learns the letters and the words that are used repeatedly in the sentence pattern. In the second book the student moves from building his knowledge of letters and single words to parts of sentences. The sentences, although they embody many repetitions, are combined to tell interesting stories about the Hill family or convey information (e.g., safe working conditions in a factory). In the third book students are taught diacritical markings to enable them to pronounce words as well as recognize them in print. At this point, sentences are combined into paragraphs, giving the students the experience of reading complete passages. In the remaining books the students continue to learn phonic rules deductively with copious examples. In the last book the emphasis is upon story reading.

YES 1. materials have an adult appearance

YES 2. covers do not mark the owners as illiterates

YES 3. contents reflect adult tastes and interests

NO 4. contents reflect adult basic education need for acculturation and re-socialization

NO 5. presents problems of social maintenance as filling in forms, keeping accounts, making time purchases

NO 6. presents citizenship or civic responsibility content

NO 7. presents problems of social adjustment

NO 8. presents special information such as technical content suitable for specific trades or job descriptions

NO 9. suitable for English as a second literate language class

NO 10. placement test(s) included in materials

YES 13. materials programed

NO 14. includes practice reading materials

NO 17. program difficult for adults

YES 18. sequentially organized skill building

YES 19. includes phonic skill training

YES 20. includes context skill training

NO 21. includes word analysis skills by word form

NO 22. includes dictionary skills

NO 23. includes other fact locating skills such as reading telephone directories

NO 24. includes map or graph reading training

YES 25. includes list of vocabulary introduced

YES 26. vocabulary taken from a standard frequency list such as the Lorge or Mitzel list

NO 27. vocabulary list analyzed according to frequency by standard list (note: #26): how many taken from 1st 500, etc.

YES 28. includes teaching manual

NO 29. manual includes lesson plans

NO 30. manual includes teaching methods

NO 31. manual describes organization of material

YES 32. provides means for self-evaluation

YES 33. self-evaluation is frequent

YES 34. self-evaluation is part of learning program

YES 35. includes handwriting training and practice

NO 36. includes speech training and practice

YES 37. pupil works mainly by himself with minimum of teacher help

NO 38. group work supports the effort of individual

NO 39. materials have been field tested

YES 43. illustrations augment instruction

YES 44. illustrations are tasteful

YES 45. illustrations are clearly and unambiguously related to text

YES 46. materials are durable

YES 47. materials are inexpensive

YES 48. materials are consumable

YES 49. style of type is pleasing

YES 50. layout design is pleasing

• *Steck-Vaughn Company*

• ADULT READER, 1964
  M. S. ROBERTSON

The *Adult Reader* is a single volume, in which reading is taught by whole words and sentences. The material is not programed, and no time allotments are suggested.

Stories of increasing difficulty about one family are presented, followed by comprehension questions for each story. Word study consists mainly of learning to recognize words by sight. The student is given practice in cursive writing only. "Work Pages" of exercises and check tests for reading and handwriting are given throughout the book. There are no lesson plans, nor is there a teacher's manual.

YES   1. materials have an adult appearance

YES   2. covers do not mark the owners as illiterates

YES   3. contents reflect adult tastes and interests

NO   4. contents reflect adult basic education need for acculturation and re-socialization

NO   5. presents problems of social maintenance as filling in forms, keeping accounts, making time purchases

NO   6. presents citizenship or civic responsibility content

NO   7. presents problems of social adjustment

NO . 8. presents special information such as technical content suitable for specific trades or job descriptions

NO   9. suitable for English as a second literate language class

NO   10. placement test(s) included in materials

NO   13. materials programed

YES   14. includes practice reading materials

YES   15. practice readings are short

YES   16. practice reading includes comprehension questions

NO   17. program difficult for adults

NO   18. sequentially organized skill building

NO   19. includes phonic skill training

NO   20. includes context skill training

NO   21. includes word analysis skills by word form

NO   22. includes dictionary skills

YES   23. includes other fact locating skills such as reading telephone directories

NO   24. includes map or graph reading training

YES   25. includes list of vocabulary introduced

NO   26. vocabulary taken from a standard frequency list such as the Lorge or Mitzel list

NO	28.	includes teaching manual
YES	32.	provides means for self-evaluation
YES	33.	self-evaluation is frequent
YES	34.	self-evaluation is part of learning program
YES	35.	includes handwriting training and practice
NO	36.	includes speech training and practice
NO	37.	pupil works mainly by himself with minimum of teacher help
YES	38.	group work supports the effort of individual
NO	39.	materials have been field tested
NO	43.	illustrations augment instruction
YES	44.	illustrations are tasteful
NO	45.	illustrations are clearly and unambiguously related to text
YES	46.	materials are durable
YES	47.	materials are inexpensive
YES	48.	materials are consumable
YES	49.	style of type is pleasing
YES	50.	layout design is pleasing

• I WANT TO READ AND WRITE, 1965
HARLEY A. SMITH AND IDA LEE KING WILBERT

The general approach taken in this single volume is through whole words and sentences. However, some word analysis skills are taught as the instruction progresses. The material is not programed, and time limits are not established for finishing the book.

The book includes a series of passages about social and economic topics, with sight words listed for each story. Oral discussion of the pictures and topics is encouraged, although no lesson plans for the teacher are given. Consonants are stressed as the primary cues in word recognition. Review lessons and tests are included. Practice is given in the mechanics of cursive writing as well as in the preparation of short compositions. The students are taught to write letters and checks.

YES   1. materials have an adult appearance

NO   2. covers do not mark the owners as illiterates

YES   3. contents reflect adult tastes and interests

NO   4. contents reflect adult basic education need for acculturation and re-socialization

YES   5. presents problems of social maintenance as filling in forms, keeping accounts, making time purchases

NO   6. presents citizenship or civic responsibility content

NO   7. presents problems of social adjustment

NO   8. presents special information such as technical content suitable for specific trades of job descriptions

NO   9. suitable for English as a second literate language class

NO   10. placement test(s) included in materials

NO   13. materials programed

YES   14. includes practice reading materials

YES   15. practice readings are short

NO   16. practice reading includes comprehension questions

NO   17. program difficult for adults

YES   18. sequentially organized skill building

YES   19. includes phonic skill training

NO   20. includes context skill training

YES   21. includes word analysis skills by word form

NO   22. includes dictionary skills

NO   23. includes other fact locating skills such as reading telephone directories

NO   24. includes map or graph reading training

YES   25. includes list of vocabulary introduced

NO   26. vocabulary taken from a standard frequency list such as Lorge or Mitzel list

NO   28. includes teaching manual

YES   32. provides means for self-evaluation

YES   33. self-evaluation is frequent

YES   34. self-evaluation is part of learning program

YES   35. includes handwriting training and practice

NO   36. includes speech training and practice

NO 37. pupil works mainly by himself with minimum of teacher help

YES 38. group work supports the effort of individual

NO 39. materials have been field tested

NO 43. illustrations augment instruction

YES 44. illustrations are tasteful

NO 45. illustrations are clearly and unambiguously related to text

YES 45. materials are durable

YES 46. materials are inexpensive

YES 48. materials are consumable

YES 49. style of type is pleasing

YES 50. layout design is pleasing

· STEPS TO LEARNING, BOOK 1 AND BOOK 2, 1965

THE EDITORIAL STAFF: BURTON W. KREITLOW, CONSULTANT

This two-volume series of workbooks is useful for either class or small-group instruction. Lessons combine reading, writing, and arithmetic instruction. Sight word recognition is taught first, but phonic and structural analysis skills are also developed. A variety of practice activities are provided, including simple arithmetic problems, alphabetizing, and completion of commonly used forms. Review lessons are frequent. Cursive writing is taught in Book 1, printing in Book 2. This reverses the sequence typically followed with children, but with adults it makes good sense: the adult learns immediately to use "adult looking" letter forms and later learns the manuscript forms.

A list of all words introduced in each volume is provided. Placement within the program is difficult for there are no provisions for an entrance test; nor is a teacher's manual provided. It may be desirable to supplement the series with additional skill builders if the program aspires to more than basic competency. The series will require a competent literacy instructor as teacher. The format probably would appeal to a young adult audience.

YES	1. materials have an adult appearance
YES	2. covers do not mark the owners as illiterates
YES	3. contents reflect adult tastes and interests
YES	4. contents reflect adult basic education need for ac-culturation and re-socialization
YES	5. presents problems of social maintenance as filling in forms, keeping accounts, making time purchases
NO	6. presents citizenship or civic responsibility content
NO	7. presents problems of social adjustment
NO	8. presents special information such as technical content suitable for specific trades or job descriptions
NO	9. suitable for English as a second literate language class
NO	10. placement test(s) included in materials
NO	13. materials programed
YES	14. includes practice reading materials
YES	15. practice readings are short
NO	16. practice reading includes comprehension questions
NO	17. program difficult for adults
YES	18. sequentially organized skill building
YES	19. includes phonic skill training
NO	20. includes context skill training
YES	21. includes word analysis skills by word form
YES	22. includes dictionary skills
NO	23. includes other fact locating skills such as reading telephone directories
NO	24. includes map or graph reading training
YES	25. includes list of vocabulary introduced
NO	26. vocabulary taken from a standard frequency list such as the Lorge or Mitzel list
NO	28. includes teaching manual
YES	32. provides means for self-evaluation
YES	33. self-evaluation is frequent
YES	34. self-evaluation is part of learning program
YES	35. includes handwriting training and practice
NO	36. includes speech training and practice

NO 37. pupil works mainly by himself with minimum of teacher help

YES 38. group work supports the effort of individual

NO 39. materials have been field tested

YES 43. illustrations augment instruction

YES 44. illustrations are tasteful

YES 45. illustrations are clearly and unambiguously related to text

YES 46. materials are durable

YES 47. materials are inexpensive

YES 48. materials are consumable

YES 49. style of type is pleasing

YES 50. layout design is pleasing

LIST II

Supplementary Skill Builders

List II includes items useful for augmenting reading skill development in an adult basic reading program. Some of the items should prove useful for aiding the development of word attack and word recognition skills; others are for the purpose of extending comprehension and interpretation abilities. The same general comments can be made about the supplementary skill builders as about reading programs. In form, style and content they should be appropriate for adult literacy classes. It is particularly important that adults who need more practice, and who consequently will need to utilize these additional materials, should have access to them. Titles of series appear in capital letters.

· *Allied Educational Council*

· THE FITZHUGH PLUS PROGRAM, 1966
LOREN AND KATHLEEN FITZHUGH

The purpose of the sections pertaining to reading skills in the Language and Numbers Series is to develop perceptual readiness for reading and to build a basic sight vocabulary. The material is programed and moves at a slow rate, with much repetition. It should be used only with complete non-readers or with students who are mentally retarded, brain-damaged, or emotionally disturbed.

· _American Southern Publishing Company_

Manuscript for Adults, Book I
Lalia Phippe Boone

Using six basic strokes, the adult learns to print correctly. He completes simple sentences by supplying missing words, which provides practice in both reading and handwriting for the beginning reader.

· _California Test Bureau_

· Lessons for Self-Instruction in Basic Skills, 1963
   Dr. Wayne F. Rosenoff, Project Coordinator

These programmed materials are intended to supplement any self-contained reading program. The branched program refers the learner for additional work when he makes an incorrect response. The student keeps his own records, so that a minimum of teacher supervision is required. The program was written for children and is somewhat juvenile in appearance, but it may be used with adults. A _Manual for Teachers_ is available; this is mainly an explanation of how the program operates.

· _Detroit Public Schools_
   Division of School Relations and
      Special Services
   Detroit Public Schools
   Detroit, Michigan

Basic Reading Skills, 1965
Peggie F. Jones and Alice Adams
Written for the Manpower Development and Training Program in Detroit, this paperback workbook focuses on teaching pre-reading skills and on building a small sight vocabulary.

After learning to print his name, address, and telephone number, the student practices visual discrimination of pictures and letters and reads some simple sentences related to work. Continued practice in printing is provided.

• DETROIT PUBLIC SCHOOLS MIMEOGRAPHED PROGRAMS
GORDON KELLER, PROGRAM WRITER

Written for the Manpower Development and Training Program, the mimeographed programs include the following titles: *On My Way to an 8-Hour Vocation, Alphabet Discrimination, Application for Employment, Starting Fractions,* and *Supplements to LET'S READ.* Although some references are made to Detroit, the programs could be used elsewhere as supplementary exercises or as guides for making up materials suitable to a particular area.

• *Educational Reading Aids Publishing Corporation*
(Cenco Educational Aids)

• YOU CAN READ, 1966

The complete package includes a pacer, a workbook, and a teacher's guide. Rolls or programs are inserted into the pacer, which controls the rate of speed (reading rate) at which the material is revealed. The publisher claims that beginning instruction is at the early third-grade level, and that by completion of the program the successful student is reading at the advanced fourth-grade level. The program begins with a roll of instruction on various aspects of the dictionary. Phonics and structural analysis exercises and stories of increasing length that are adult in content are given later. Frequent reviews and comprehension tests on the stories are included.

• *Field Enterprises*

• THE CYCLO-TEACHER

The Cyclo-Teacher is a flat, circular device. The student writes his answers to questions on the program, and the answers appear when the program is advanced to the next slot. Only one student may use the device at a time. Although many programs are available, those most likely to be useful in a literacy class would be *Using Letters in Words,* designed to develop phonic skills, and the language arts cycles.

- *Jack Hood School Supplies Company, Ltd.*

- CHECK AND DOUBLE CHECK PUPILS' WORKBOOK IN PHONICS, 1963

Although these workbooks are intended for children, they may — with the probable exception of the first level book, which is too juvenile in format and content — to be used with newly literate adults. Phonics rules are presented deductively, with copious examples, exercises and illustrative drawings. Frequent tests are provided to ensure that the student has learned the material. No initial test is given because the student is assumed to have no knowledge of phonics skills.

- ENGLISH REVIEW AND PRACTICE TESTS

Although the tests are intended for use with children in September to determine retention from the studies of the previous year, they could be used in adult basic education classes as the material is taught. In addition to English usage, the tests also measure reading and writing skills. The tests are valuable in that they can provide a rough guide to the functioning of students as well as measure knowledge of skills.

- *The King Company*

You Can Read, 1956
Alice Kirkpatrick McMichael

First the student studies the difference in sound between the long and short vowels through association with drawings; then he learns the consonant sounds in different positions in the word. The format, although somewhat childish, would probably be acceptable to adults for supplementary work.

Conquests in Reading, 1962
William Kottmeyer and Kay Ware

The workbook includes reading selections and exercises that enable the student to acquire phonics and structural analysis skills rapidly. Although the book is intended for children, it may be used as a supplement in an adult reading program. The *Teacher's Edition* provides background teaching aids and a list of supplementary materials.

· New Practice Readers, 1962
  Donald G. Anderson, Ardis Edwards Burton, Charles C. Grover, and Clarence R. Stone

Although these readers are intended for children, they could be used in an adult literacy class. The factual stories are followed by questions that test comprehension of specific facts, implications, and the main idea. Vocabulary study is given both before and after the stories.

Step Up Your Reading Power, Book A, 1966
Jim Olson

Book A is written at the third- and fourth-grade reading levels, according to the label in the front cover of the book. Short reading selections about hygiene, job-hunting and other important subjects are followed by comprehension questions.

· *Modern Curriculum Press*

· Phonics Is Fun, 1963
  Louis Krane

The three books in the series were written for children, but they can be used with adults who are beginning readers.

Each page forms a self-contained unit, with the topic identified at the top of the page. Much practice and frequent review are provided. Association of sounds with the names of pictured objects is the most-used instrumental technique. A *Teacher's Manual* is provided for each book.

· *Noble and Noble Publishers, Inc.*

Everyday English and Basic Word List for Adults, 1964
Angelica W. Cass

The purpose of the book is to teach a basic word list through stories. First the student studies a list of words with the teacher's help and then he reads a story in which they are used. Although the student is given some phonics rules, the approach is essentially through the whole word; phonics skills are not applied in the book although the teacher may choose to do so on his own. Practical information is given. For example, the students learn how to write letters and fill out forms.

Write Your Own Letters, 1964
Jeannette B. Rosenfeld and Angelica W. Cass

In this book students are given forms to follow in writing various kinds of letters. Likewise, the book provides a model content for certain types of letters, such as invitations, excuses for absence and letters of sympathy. Students are also told how to send a telegram and write a check.

· *F. A. Owen Publishing Company*

· CHARTS

By stick figure illustrations and simple, easy-reading sentences the student learns some tips in the areas of health, manners and safety. In addition to conveying content, the charts can be used for practice reading at the beginning level.

- *Peterson Handwriting System*
- HANDWRITING LEGIBILITY KIT, 1966

The student first learns to print and then to write by using colors to distinguish a new stroke from the part of the letter that he has already learned to form. The kit is self-instructional if the student can read the directions. If he cannot, he can follow the directional arrows with the teacher's help. The kit is definitely adult in orientation, and it contains sample forms, such as a Job Corps application, a voter registration form, a personal check and the income tax short form.

- *Reader's Digest Services, Inc.*
- READING SKILL BUILDERS

These supplementary skill builders were written for children and include four books at the first-grade level and three books at the second- through sixth-grade levels. The format is such that even the lower-level books would be reasonably palatable to adults. The books include articles and stories that may be used for supplementary reading. Skill-building activities, which follow the articles, include exercises in phonics, structural analysis, comprehension and vocabulary development. Word counts are given for the most articles, so they can readily be used for practice in speed reading. A *Teacher's Edition* is available for each book.

- *Science Research Associates*
- NEW ROCHESTER OCCUPATIONAL READING SERIES, 1965
  HERMAN R. GOLDBERG AND WINIFRED T. BRUMBER

The text book for the series, *The Job Ahead*, is available at three difficulty levels, ranging from very easy to intermediate grade-level difficulty. Workbooks are available at each level. A *Teacher's Manual* provides lesson plans and word lists for each level of difficulty. The exercises include

vocabulary development, word study, comprehension questions, phonics skills, practical mathematics, questions geared
to personal guidance, and other information essential to the
adult such as job interviewing and completing income tax
forms.

· *George Wahr Publishing Company*

Remedial Reading Drills, Revised, 1965
Drs. Thorleif G. Hegge, Samuel A. Kirk, and Winifred
D. Kirk

Although the book was originally intended for children —
particularly slow learners — there are no pictures, so it has
an adult appearance. The book includes a series of phonics
drills. Consonant substitution is used extensively. Diphthongs,
blends and phonograms are presented.

LIST III
Supplementary Reading Materials

The selected list of supplementary readings that follows is
short, mainly because the incentive to publish in this field is
fairly recent. Few, if any, adequately reflect the general aim
of adult education, which is to stimulate the student's interest
in himself and to help him find a deeper insight into the
problems of life as an individual or as a member of society.
Adult basic education and adult education should have the
same fundamental goal: to incorporate the mature individual
into the broad social sphere. The aim of adult basic education
should not be merely to make the individual fit for employment.

The world of the illiterate ought to be reflected in the materials he will first meet in print. If he expects this, he will be
generally disappointed by their superficiality and their lack
of seriousness. He may also note the similarity between easy
reading materials for adults and materials for children.

Most of the supplementary readings do not contain a list
of words used. This makes it difficult for the teacher to assess

their usefulness accurately. Grade level estimates, where they appear, are inaccurate guides to reading difficulty, and grade level itself is no guarantee that the materials will be compatible with grade levels designated in the various programs.

Titles of series appear in capital letters.

· *Fearon Publishers, Inc.*

· To Be a Good American Series, 1965
MARGARET W. HUDSON AND ANN A. WEAVER

Although the series is intended for junior or senior high school students in classes for slow learners or the educable mentally retarded, it may be used with English-speaking or foreign-born adults who have some literacy skills. Included in the series are the following: Book 1: *In Your Family*, Book 2: *In Your Community*, Book 3: *In Your State*, and Book 4: *In Your Country*. The pages are removable to permit the teacher to use the book as he wishes. A manual, which includes a list of suggested supplementary activities, is available.

· *Follet Publishing Company*

· Accent Education (in press)

The emphasis of the series is upon resocialization and personal guidance. New words are listed at the beginning of the selections and introductory questions are presented. The student is encouraged to use the new words in his own sentences and to study the guide questions. After reading a selection, the student answers questions that are aimed at personal guidance rather than at testing comprehension.

· *Garrard Publishing Company*

· Discovery Books
DR. MARY C. AUSTIN, EDITOR

This series of books, written at an easy (third-grade) reading level, comprises well illustrated biographies of famous people.

The books were written for children, but they probably would be palatable to adults.

Folklore of the World Books

The folklore and myths of various countries are told in attractively illustrated cloth-bound books. The books were written for children, on the third-grade reading level.

• *The George Washington University*

The Automobile, 1965

Descriptions of the different models of cars are written in short sentences. Pictures help to convey the meaning of the technical vocabulary. Although the book does contain some difficult words and concepts, it would be possible for the beginning adult reader who was quite familiar with cars to read the book with help.

• *Government Printing Office*

• BECOMING A CITIZEN SERIES, 1965

Included in the series are: Book 1: *Our American Way of Life;* Book 2: *Our United States;* Book 3: *Our Government.* Although the series begins with a whole-word approach, the lessons move very rapidly, allowing little practice. Writing is not taught, but opportunity for practice is provided. Oral discussion is also encouraged, making the series especially valuable for foreign-born students. Books 2 and 3 would be useful, with help from the teacher, in explaining how the American community works. Comprehension questions, vocabulary development and discussion questions are provided at the end of each reading selection.

• PAMPHLETS FROM THE CHILDREN'S BUREAU

Written in simple English and well illustrated to convey meaning, these pamphlets discuss various aspects of child care. Two pamphlets, for example, are *When Your Baby is on the Way* and *Your Baby's First Year.*

· PAMPHLETS FROM THE DEPARTMENT OF AGRICULTURE

Free or inexpensive pamphlets are available on a variety of topics. They are written in simple sentences and elementary vocabulary. Some titles that may serve as samples are the following: *Eat a Good Breakfast; Removing Stains From Fabrics; First Aid for Flooded Homes and Farms;* and *Food for Families with School Children.*

· SANITATION SERIES: FEDERAL EXTENSION SERVICE

Written in simple English, the pamphlets cover topics relating mainly to hygiene. The essential points are well illustrated by diagrams and drawings, by which meaning is conveyed. Some sample titles are *Drink Safe Water, How to Wash Your Clothes, Personal Cleanliness,* and *Wash Dishes Right.*

Stories Worth Knowing and *Stories for Today*
Edgar Dale

Prepared for use with members of the armed forces, these paperback books contain short stories on a variety of subjects, not necessarily relating to the military life. The key words are listed before each story and comprehension questions follow.

· *Holt, Rinehart, and Winston, Inc.*

Get Your Money's Worth, 1965
Aurelia Toyer

This story of a family that moves to the city includes many facts for consumers. Discussion questions are included.

Life with the Lucketts, 1965
Phyllis D. Morris

This is the story of an urban family that encounters a typical problem of city life when Mr. Luckett loses his job because of automation and must seek a new one. Discussion questions follow each chapter to test comprehension orally and to involve the students in the story. New words are given at the end of each chapter and at the end of the book. The book is paperback and not illustrated.

The Thomases Live Here, 1965
Jocelyn Pretlow Goss

A paperback and part of the FIRST SERIES, the book is intended to be used as supplementary reading material with _Learning to Read and Write._ The new words are listed at the end of each chapter and again at the back of the book. There are no illustrations. The Thomases are a low-income rural family whose problems may be like those of some beginning adult readers. At the end of each chapter are discussion questions that project the students into the situations described in the book.

Measure, Cut, and Sew, 1965
Johnetta Starks

Although no word lists are included, comprehension questions are given at the end of each chapter and the book is illustrated to help convey the meaning. The book is written in simple sentences that outline the steps in sewing.

• _Institutional Book Service_

• FRONTIERS OF AMERICAN BOOKS

This hardback series relates true stories from history. The books were written for children, on a third-grade level of difficulty.

· *Koinonia Foundation*

· PAMPHLETS FROM THE KOINONIA FOUNDATION

Pamphlets on a variety of subjects are written on three levels, based on the Lorge-Thorndike Word List. The books are illustrated so that the central meaning is conveyed through drawings, and new words are listed for study. Some of the titles are: *A Boy and His Plants: A Story of George Washington Carver; A Dream Comes True; Eating is Fun; and Going to Have a Baby?*

· *Lerner Publications Company*

They Wouldn't Quit
Ravina Gelfand and Letha Patterson

In fairly elementary language the stories of handicapped people are related. The book has an attractive cloth cover, but the illustrations do not convey essential meanings. An adult with limited reading experience would probably be able to read the book with some help.

· *McGraw-Hill Book Company*

Our Constitution and What It Means, Third Edition (Simplified), 1965
William A. Kottmeyer

The federal constitution is printed with notes of explanation and definition. This paperback book is well illustrated to convey the essential meaning, so the beginning adult reader could probably read it with help. A list of words and their definitions is provided at the back of the book.

· *New Readers Press*

The First Christmas Tree, 1961
Grace Bowman

The story is presented in simple sentences, printed one per line. The beginning adult might need some help with the difficult words, but the story is familiar and probably appealing.

Good Manners in the United States, 1961
Bengt Simonsson and Earl Roe

This small paperback book outlines proper behavior in certain situations. Although the book contains helpful illustrations that convey meaning, the student might need help with the reading task.

Heroes of Faith, 1959
Robert S. Laubach, Editor

This book is intended for adults who have completed _Stream-lined English,_ Revised, Part I. The words used are based on _Streamlined English Word Lists._ The introduction of new words is controlled, and they are listed at the end of each story.

How to Find a Job, 1959
Robert Francis and Sam Iftikhar

Suggestions are made about applying and interviewing for jobs. A sample application form is provided for practice.

News for You

A weekly newspaper, _News for You,_ appears in two editions. Edition A is on the third reading level in the Laubach program, and Edition B is on the fourth. The paper not only covers the events of the week but also conveys important information about matters like health insurance and provides entertainment in crossword puzzles. The two editions could be used in a classroom where reading abilities vary, because both editions cover similar content. A _Teacher's Guide_ is available.

Our United States, 1965

A short description of each of the states and territories is presented in this large paperback book. A glossary of difficult words is included in the back of the book. With a teacher's help, the book could be read by a beginning adult reader.

Our World is Small, 1964

International understanding is taught through pictures. The beginning adult reader should have no trouble reading this small paperback book, for the only reading material is in the form of one-sentence captions.

· THE STORY OF JESUS, 1946
  FRANK C. LAUBACH

The three parts in the series are the following: *Jesus' Birth and Ministry; Jesus' Death and Resurrection;* and *The Parables of Jesus.* The beginning stories are printed in short sentences, one per line. At the end of the first book the Bible stories are printed in paragraph form. The stories continue, becoming progressively more difficult. New words are listed at the beginning of each story and at the end of each book.

Trouble and the Police, 1959
Nicholas Titus and Negash Gebremarian

In this small paperback book a conversation between two policemen and two citizens focuses upon various types of crimes and punishments. Although no vocabulary list is included, the words seem elementary and the illustrations convey much of the meaning.

We Honor Them, I and II, 1964–1965
Willie Mae Watson

These two illustrated paper back volumes contain short stories about outstanding Negroes. Words not listed in the Thorndike-Lorge and Laubach lists are defined at the back of Volume I and listed at the back of Volume II. Word games and supplementary activities are provided.

Why You Need Insurance, 1959
George Gillespie and George Wanyee

Through a story of a family, different kinds of insurance are discussed. Although short, simple sentences are used, the student might need some help in reading the book because there are not many illustrations to aid in conveying meaning.

· _Noble and Noble Publishers, Inc._

How to Become a United States Citizen, 1963
Angelica W. Cass

Citizenship information is printed in numbered sentences, followed by comprehension questions, word study, simple grammatical concepts, and supplementary activities. A word list is included in the back of the book.

Live and Learn, 1962
Angelica W. Cass

Although the reading level is not prescribed, this book assumes some ability to read and write. The students first read a story and then answer questions to build comprehension skills, sight vocabulary and knowledge of grammatical usage. Word attack skills are not taught.

The subject matter is likely to be of interest to both foreign-born and native Americans adults, for the book includes both procedures for acquiring citizenship and general information.

Family Life in the U.S.A., 1962

Comprehension questions, work on usage, sight vocabulary words, and oral discussion are provided for following selections. The student must possess some reading skill to use the book effectively.

· *Public Affairs Pamphlets*

· PUBLIC AFFAIRS PAMPHLETS

These inexpensive pamphlets, written at an easy reading level, convey pertinent information on a variety of subjects. Examples of the topics available include the following: *Buyer, Be Wary! Your Health Is Your Business; Smoking — The Great Dilemma; Parents' Guide to Children's Vision;* and *How to S-T-R-E-T-C-H Your Money.*

· *Random House School and Library Service, Inc.*

· EASY-TO-READ BOOKS

This series for children, written on a third-grade reading level, includes books on a variety of scientific subjects. The books are attractively illustrated.

· *Reader's Digest Services, Inc.*

· ADULT READERS

The books in the series are divided into three reading levels, all within the basic reading range. Skill-development exercises are included after each story. The books are well illustrated and appealing, with a general format that is similar to the *Reader's Digest.* An outline of the reading skills developed in each set of exercises and a discussion of the theme of each story are presented in the *Teacher's Manual.*

· THE SCIENCE READERS

The articles, although intended to develop interest in science, also include work on comprehension skills, such as observing, obtaining facts, and drawing conclusions. The first book — *Green Book* — is at the basic level.

• *Regents' Publishing Company*

• THE U.S.A. READERS

The first book in the series — *The Land and the People* — has a vocabulary range of 1,200 words. The book is sparsely illustrated, but simple sentences are used to aid the new reader. After each chapter, in which the history and geography of a part of the United States is discussed, conversation and vocabulary exercises, which also serve as comprehension checks, are given.

• *Frank E. Richards, Publisher*

Foundations of Citizenship
Bernard Shawn

This cloth-bound book is in two volumes, which are bound together, with a duplicate word list at the back of each. The content covers a variety of topics, such as finding a job, evaluating student interests, budgeting, taxation, and suggestions for social conduct. The discussion questions emphasize good citizenship practices both within and outside the family. Although the reading material is fairly difficult for the beginning reader, the book may be used with teacher help. The illustrations also convey the crux of the stories. No suggestions for the teacher are given.

• THE GETTING ALONG SERIES, 1963
THOMAS MOONEY

The reading instruction that is provided is by the whole-word approach. The emphasis of the series, however, is upon good personal habits and citizenship. The books are especially oriented toward the interests of high-school age students. Some ability to read and write is assumed, for the students begin by studying spelling and correct usage. After reading a story of considerable length, which includes pre-studied words, they answer written and discussion questions that not only test comprehension of the story but also encourage good citizenship practices.

Happy Housekeepers, 1964
Helen R. Prevo

The book may be used as practice reading material for women, especially those of high school age. The stories are followed by comprehension and discussion questions and supplementary activities. The content emphasizes household hygiene, etiquette, and maintenance. Some reading ability is required.

LIST IV
U.S. Government Printing Office Publications

There are approximately 25,000 different factual publications currently available for sale from the Government Printing Office. Many of them are simply enough written and yet contain the type of usable technical information to suit the interests and needs of beginning adult readers. They can be used to supplement a skill-building program. Pamphlets are published on a wide variety of topics, such as consumer information, hygiene, agriculture, and forestry. Subject lists of publications are available from the Superintendent of Documents upon request. The lists are revised annually.

The great majority of the items listed are relatively inexpensive. New literates should be encouraged to build a library of personal reference materials for themselves. Teachers may be able to make some of the pamphlets available as needed, or they may encourage students to purchase their own.

Two service publications are also available from the Superintendent of Documents: a free bi-weekly list of selected U.S. Government Publications and a monthly catalog of all publications, both of which may be purchased on an annual basis for $4.50.

50.   American History
38.   Animal Industry
        Farm Animals, poultry and dairying
19.   Army
        Field manuals and technical manuals
84.   Atomic Energy and Civil Defense
79.   Aviation
        Civil aviation, naval aviation, Air Force, National
        Aeronautics and Space Administration, technical
        reports and space
70.   Census
        Statistics of agriculture, business, governments, hous-
        ing, manufactures, minerals, population, and maps
71.   Children's Bureau, and other publications relating to
        children and youth
62.   Commerce
        Business, patents, trademarks, and foreign trade
86.   Consumer Information
        Family finances, appliances, recreation, gardening,
        health and safety, food, house and home, child care,
        and clothing and fabrics
85.   Defense
        Veterans' affairs
51A. Diseases
        Contagious and infectious diseases, sickness, and vital
        statistics
31.   Education
68.   Farm Management
        Foreign agriculture, rural electrification, agricultural
        marketing
28.   Finance
        National economy, accounting, insurance, securities
21.   Fish and Wildlife
65.   Foreign Relations of U.S.
43.   Forestry
        Managing and using forest and range land, includ-

ing timber and lumber, ranges and grazing, American woods

15. Geology
36. Government Periodicals and Subscription Services
60. Guam, Puerto Rico, Samoa, and Virgin Islands
51. Health, and Hygiene
    Drugs and sanitation
72. Homes
    Construction, maintenance, community development
11. Home Economics
    Foods and cooking
67. Immigration, Naturalization, and Citizenship
55. Indians
    Smithsonian Institution. Fine Arts Commission, Archeology, ethnology
41. Insects
    Worms and insects harmful to man, animals, and plants
59. Interstate Commerce
42. Irrigation, Drainage, and Water Power
10. Laws, Rules, and Regulations
83. Library of Congress
53. Maps
    Engineering, Surveying
58. Mines
    Explosives, fuel, gasoline, gas petroleum, minerals
35. National Parks
    Historic Sites, National Monuments
63. Navy
    Marine Corps and Coast Guard
33A. Occupations
    Professions and job descriptions
44. Plants
    Culture, grading, marketing, and storage of fruits, vegetables, grass and grain

54. Political Science
    Government, crime, District of Columbia
81. Posters and Charts
82. Radio and Electricity
    Electronics, radar, communications
64. Scientific Tests, Standards
    Mathematics, physics
78. Social Security
    Industrial hazards, health and hygiene, pensions, safety for workers, workmen's compensation and insurance
46. Soils and Fertilizers
    Soil surveys, erosion, conservation
37. Tariff and Taxation
25. Transportation
    Highways, Roads, Postal Service
48. Weather, Astronomy, Meteorology

LIST V

Materials for Teaching Reading to Foreign-Born Adults*

Affiliated Publishers, Inc.

FIRST STEPS IN READING ENGLISH, Christine M. Gibson and I. A. Richards, 1959.

English Through Pictures, Christine M. Gibson and I. A. Richards, 1965.

A First Workbook of English, Christine M. Gibson and I. A. Richards, 1965.

Silver Burdett Company

ENGLISH: YOUR NEW LANGUAGE, in press

Collier-Macmillan International

ENGLISH 900, English Language Services, Inc., 1946

ENGLISH THIS WAY, English Language Services, Inc., 1964

* Titles of series are capitalized; single books are italicized.

Fearon Publishers, Inc.
TO BE A GOOD AMERICAN SERIES, Margaret W. Hudson and
  Ann A. Weaver, 1965

Government Printing Office
BECOMING A CITIZEN SERIES, 1965
OUR CONSTITUTION AND GOVERNMENT, 1965

Houghton Mifflin Company
LEARNING THE ENGLISH LANGUAGE, English Language Research, Inc., 1963

McGraw-Hill Book Company
ENGLISH FOR TODAY, National Council of Teachers of English, 1962.
Our Constitution and What it Means, Third Edition (Simplified), William A. Kottmeyer, 1965.

Noble and Noble Publishers, Inc.
Live and Learn, Angelica W. Cass, 1962
How to Become a United States Citizen, Angelica W. Cass,
  1963
Family Life in the U.S.A., Gladys Alesi and Dora Pantell,
  1962
The Story of Our America, Orrel T. Baldwin, 1964
English Step by Step — With Pictures, Ralph S. Boggs and
  Robert J. Dixson, 1965
COMPLETE COURSE IN ENGLISH, Robert J. Dixson

Reader's Digest Services, Inc.
READER'S DIGEST READINGS

Regents Publishing Company, Inc.
English Step by Step — With Pictures, Ralph S. Boggs and
  Robert J. Dixson, 1965
COMPLETE COURSE IN ENGLISH, Robert J. Dixson
English in Action, Robert J. Dixson
LEARNING TO USE ENGLISH, Mary Finocchario

Beginning Lessons in English, Isobel Y. Fisher and Robert J. Dixson

Second Book in English, Robert J. Dixson

MODERN AMERICAN ENGLISH SERIES, Robert J. Dixson

The U.S.A. Readers

AMERICAN CLASSICS, Robert J. Dixson

Family Life in the U.S.A., Gladys Alesi and Dora Pantell, 1962

Elementary Reader in English, Robert J. Dixson

Easy Reading Selections in English, Robert J. Dixson

Frank E. Richards, Publisher
Foundations of Citizenship, Bernard Shawn, 1965

Steck-Vaughn Company
I Want To Learn English, Revised, Harley A. Smith and Ida Lee King Wilbert, 1965
Learning and Writing English, Revised, M. S. Robertson, 1964
My Country, Revised, Edwin H. Smith and Florence R. Lutz, 1964

LIST VI
A Selected List of Publications Useful to Literacy Instructors

Alesi, Gladys, and Mary C. McDonald. *Teaching Illiterate Adults To Read: College-Adult Reading Instruction* (Perspectives in Reading No. 1). Newark, Delaware: International Reading Association, 1964.

Free and Inexpensive Learning Materials, 1966–1967 ed., Nashville: George Peabody College for Teachers, 1966.

Gray, William S. *The Teaching of Reading and Writing.* Chicago: Scott, Foresman and Company, 1961.

Greenleigh Associates. *Education Rehabilitation: An Evaluation of the Adult Basic Education Program of the State of Illinois.* New York: 1965.

Harris, Albert J. *How To Increase Reading Ability.* New York: David McKay Company, Inc., 1961.

Kottmeyer, W. *Teacher's Guide for Remedial Reading.* St. Louis: McGraw-Hill Book Company, Webster Division, 1959.

Lanning, Frank W., and Wesley A. Many. *Basic Education for the Disadvantaged Adult: Theory and Practice.* Boston: Houghton Mifflin Company, 1966.

Mott Adult Reading Center. *Teaching Adults To Read.* Galien, Michigan: Allied Education Council, 1966.

The Office of Economic Opportunity. *Catalog of Federal Programs for Individual and Community Improvement.* Washington, D.C.: The U.S. Government Printing Office, 1965.

Reissman, F. *The Culturally Deprived Child.* New York: Harper & Brothers, 1962.

Smith, Edwin M., and Marie P. Smith. *Teaching Reading to Adults.* Washington, D.C.: National Association of Public School Adult Educators, 1962.

UNESCO, International Bureau of Education. *Literacy and Education for Adults.* XXVIIth International Conference on Public Education. Geneva, 1964.

Wallace, Mary C. *Literacy Instructor's Handbook.* Chicago: Follet Publishing Company, 1965.

· PUBLISHERS' ADDRESSES

Affiliated Publishers, Inc., 630 Fifth Avenue, New York, New York 10020

Allied Education Council, P.O. Box 78, Galien, Michigan 49113

American Incentive to Read, 2015 West Olympic Boulevard, Los Angeles, California 90006

American Southern Publishing Company, P.O. Box 408, Northport, Alabama 35476

Baylor Book Store, The Literacy Center, Box 6325, Waco, Texas 76700

Behavioral Research Laboratories, Box 577, Palo Alto, California 94302

California Test Bureau, Del Monte Research Park, Monterey, California 93940

Collier-Macmillan International, 60 Fifth Avenue, New York, New York 10011

Croft Educational Services, 100 Garfield Avenue, New London, Connecticut 06301

Educational Reading Aids Publishing Corp., Cenco Educational Aids, Carle Place, Long Island, New York 11100

Encyclopedia Britannica Press, Inc., 425 North Michigan Avenue, Chicago, Illinois 60611

Fearon Publishers, Inc., 2165 Park Boulevard, Palo Alto, California 94306

Field Enterprises Educational Corporation, 510 Merchandise Mart Plaza, Chicago, Illinois 60654

Follett Publishing Company, 1010 West Washington Boulevard, Chicago, Illinois 60607

Garrard Publishing Co., 1607 North Market Street, Champaign, Illinois 61821

Government Printing Office, c/o Superintendent of Documents, Washington, D.C. 20402

Harcourt, Brace & World, Inc., 757 Third Avenue, New York, New York 10017.

Harper & Row, Publishers, 49 East 33rd Street, New York, New York 10016

Holt, Rinehart & Winston, Inc., 383 Madison Avenue, New York, New York 10017

Jack Hood School Supplies, Ltd., 91–99 Erie Street, Stratford, Ontario, Canada

Houghton Mifflin Company, 110 Tremont Street, Boston, Massachusetts 02107

Institutional Book Service, 1224 Van Buren Street, Chicago, Illinois 60607

King Company (The), 2414 West Lawrence Avenue, Chicago, Illinois 60625

Koinonia Foundation, Box 5744, Baltimore, Maryland 21200

Lerner Publications Co., 133 First Avenue North, Minneapolis, Minnesota 55401

McGraw-Hill Book Company, Webster Division, Manchester Road, Manchester, Missouri 63011

David McKay Co., Inc., 750 Third Avenue, New York, New York 10017

Modern Curriculum Press, Berea Industrial Park, Berea, Ohio 44017

National Association of Public School Adult Educators, Washington, D.C. 20036

New Readers Press, Box 131, Syracuse, New York, 13210

Noble & Noble Publishers, Inc., 750 Third Avenue, New York, New York 10017

F. A. Owen Publishing Co., Instructor Park, Dansville, New York 14437

Peterson Handwriting System, Greensburg, Pennsylvania 15601

Public Affairs Pamphlets, 381 Park Avenue, South, New York, New York 10016

Random House School & Library Service, Inc., 457 Madison Avenue, New York, New York 10022

Reader's Digest Services, Inc., Pleasantville, New York 10570

Regents Publishing Co., Inc., 200 Park Avenue South, New York, New York 10003

Frank E. Richards, Publisher, 215 Church Street, Phoenix, New York 13135

Science Research Associates, Inc., 259 East Erie Street, Chicago, Illinois 60611

Scott, Foresman & Company, 1900 East Lake Avenue, Glenville, Illinois 60025

Silver Burdett Company, Park Avenue & Columbia Road, Morristown, New Jersey 07960

Steck-Vaughn Company, P.O. Box 2028, Austin, Texas 78767

George Wahr Publishing Company, 316 South State Street, Ann Arbor, Michigan 48103

5

IMPLEMENTING THE INSTRUCTIONAL PROGRAM

Instructional materials for adult basic reading are available, if not in profusion, at least in adequate quantity and variety to meet a wide range of instructional needs. The teacher, then, is confronted not with a general lack of materials but with the necessity of choosing the materials that will be most useful in a particular situation. There is no single set of generalizations that will serve to solve the problems of materials selection. Many things must be considered: the teacher's own preferences and skills; the unique characteristics of the group; the individual strengths and weaknesses of the pupils to be taught. Yet there are considerations that, combined with good judgment, provide guidelines for the intelligent selection of material. The basic aim in this chapter is to provide a framework for selecting materials in the belief that, particularly in adult basic reading, this task is crucial to the successful implementation of the instructional program.

• SEQUENTIAL DEVELOPMENT OF READING SKILLS

Most textbooks on the teaching of reading to elementary school children include a discussion of and an outline for the sequential teaching of reading skills. In general, there is agreement on some of the details and rather sharp disagreement on others, which results in lack of uniformity as materials are developed and skills are taught. This lack can cause difficulties for teachers as they attempt to find parallel instructional materials and for pupils as they move from one situation to another. Unfortunately, definitive research that would provide final answers to questions of optimum sequence does not exist. But a pragmatic solution to the problem can be found by accepting the sequence of skill development found in the particular materials used for reading instruction, choosing supplementary material with this sequence in mind, and making adequate provision for extra instruction when skills are interjected out of sequence.

A basic point here is that with our present knowledge it is impossible to suggest a "best" sequence of reading skill development. This is as true in teaching adults as in teaching children. It is less important to mourn this fact than to seek the guidance that is available in order to establish some guidelines. Also, what is defensible and successful with children may not be so with adults. Adults come to beginning reading instruction with backgrounds of experience, previous instruction and expectations that differ from children's; and this obvious fact cannot be ignored. Finally, if an intensive phonics approach to teaching beginning reading is chosen, the initial sequence of skill development is set by the particular phonics system employed. The approach dictates the sequence.

First Stage: Sight Words

Basal reading instruction for children typically begins — unless an intensive phonics system is used — with the introduction of a number of sight words, probably 50 to 75 of them. This practice has undoubtedly led some of the less perceptive critics of teaching methods to harangue about the fallacies of a "see-and-say" method and the charge that children are being forced to learn to read by memorizing each new word that is introduced. The fact is that to teach reading strictly through the memorization of sight words would be absurd, and it probably has never been seriously suggested. Yet the introduction of a few sight words at the very beginning makes sense:

children are very quickly able to gain satisfaction from reading short sentences, they are immediately impressed with the fact that the purpose of all reading is to get meaning, and the words serve as raw material for teaching phonic and other word analysis generalizations and skills.

This practice is probably even more defensible with adults. Even almost completely illiterate adults are likely to come to reading instruction already knowing a number of sight words, and they are eager to have the experience of actually reading connected text. Careful selection of materials that can be read or the development of "experience stories" — told by the students and written down by the teacher — can insure immediate application of existing knowledge and provide a valuable success experience. Furthermore, many functionally illiterate adults are able to convert single letters to sounds with some success, but they are unable to blend the sounds into whole words. To begin instruction with more of the same would merely add to existing frustrations.

The sight-recognition stage is the time to establish the habits of using context for word identification and always reading for comprehension. With adults there is much less need for the control of meaning vocabulary or for the development of new word meanings through readiness activities than with children, because adults will typically have relatively well developed spoken vocabularies. This stage is also the time for practice in auditory perception: students generally cannot see what they cannot say. Stressing the correct pronunciation of sight words prepares the way for the visual analysis that is to come.

This is also the time to establish the habit of left-to-right direction in approaching the reading task. Whole words combined in meaningful context contribute as the student "reads through" to get meaning. For those who have difficulty, a device like the Controlled Reader (available from Educational Developmental Laboratory, 284 Pulaski Road, Huntington, New York 11746) can be useful; the device systematically exposes lines of print in a left-to-right sequence. Pointing out similarities and differences in the beginnings and endings of words also can be helpful, and such practice serves as a transitional step toward word analysis.

Adequate practice must be provided to develop rapid, automatic recognition of important sight words. This is not to say that all words introduced as sight words should be mastered to this degree. But the reader will profit greatly from ability to recognize without hesitation the service type words that recur frequently in all printed materials. The 220 words on the Dolch (*1939*) list, which has gained wide acceptance, are examples. The key to instant word recognition is repetition. The use of tachistoscopic devices for drill in quick recognition may help to relieve monotony, but as much can be accomplished — and more economically — through the use of flash cards. The cards also offer the advantage of complete flexibility; the teacher or the students themselves can make word or phrase cards from words actually used, as they are needed. If, however, flash card drill is perceived as a childish exercise, tachistoscopic devices may add a bit of sophistication and make the drill more acceptable.

One final point is in order, although it is not related explicitly to reading instruction. Virtually all school children learn manuscript (printing) before they learn cursive (writing) handwriting. They make the transition from manuscript to cursive sometime between the middle of third and the end of fourth grade. The practice of initially introducing manuscript letter forms is defended on two bases. First, it is felt — although research evidence is scanty, at best — that manuscript letter forms are more easily handled by young children, whose fine muscle coordination is not yet fully developed. Second, it is felt — and again there is limited research support — that, because manuscript letter forms closely resemble the type used in printed materials, learning manuscript letter forms develops letter perception and discrimination, which in turn enhances achievement in both reading and spelling. Obviously, the first argument does not hold for adults, but the second seems as logical with adults as with children. Yet, more often than not the writers of adult materials suggest cursive style for beginning handwriting instruction for adults. The argument is that adults are anxious to have handwriting that looks adult and that the connected style makes for more rhythmic, flowing movement and habituation of the left-to-right movement required in writing and reading. The defense of each style for beginning instruction has a great deal of logical appeal. In the absence of clearly demonstrated superiority for either form, students and teachers ought to be free to choose the style with the most personal appeal. Actually, it is probably expedient for adults to master both styles simultaneously, or at least very early in the sequence of their emerging literacy.

Second Stage: Word Analysis

A new reader does not become truly independent from a tutor until he is able to decipher unfamiliar words — that is, words not learned as sight words — on his own. Independent reading is a decoding process. Symbols are transformed into sounds that, if they are equivalent to words in the reader's conceptual vocabulary, evoke meaning. (Much later in the skill-development sequence the reader may be able to get meaning directly from printed symbols, bypassing the intervening conversion of symbol to sound. But this is a sophisticated skill that has not been mastered by many college graduates. Teachers should not be disturbed if their newly literate pupils persist for some time in vocalizing — whispering, or at least moving their lips — while they read.) Thus, everyone agrees that readers need some system for "sounding out" words.

There is little agreement, however, concerning how a sounding system can most efficiently be taught. To say that "phonics" is the answer is to grossly oversimplify. Educators have been as guilty as laymen of speaking blithely of "phonics" as if somewhere there were golden tablets with the laws written down for all to embrace and keep inviolate for all time. But there is no paradigmatic phonics system. There are as many "phonics" as there are systems for phonics instruction. The systems differ widely. Some introduce short vowels first, some introduce long vowels first, and a few ignore vowels entirely; some present as few as four to eight principles and others list a hundred or more; some begin from a sight word base, others begin with isolated sound drills; some teach "word families," others condemn the practice. Furthermore, many children work out a personal system for breaking the sound-symbol code with but minimal phonics instruction. Adults, with their wider experience and greater ability to cope with abstractions and inconsistencies, are even more likely to succeed in working out personal systems. To insist, then, on intensive phonics instruction may be to belabor the development of skills that, for many, are not needed.

The problem of developing independence in attacking and pronouncing words is probably best solved through comprehensive instruction in *word analysis.* This includes both phonic and structural analysis, plus contextual analysis and use of the dictionary. The practical matters of specific content and sequential development of the several types of skills will be dictated largely by the materials employed. Often the skills are best taught spontaneously as needs and opportunities arise. A brief presentation of some generalizations regarding phonics and structural analysis is included here in the hope that it will contribute to the development of a framework for comprehensive instruction in word analysis.

· **Phonics.** The content of phonics instruction is determined by the particular system used. Research has not been sufficiently definitive to show which system is best. Therefore, teachers should choose materials carefully and then be prepared to live with them. But regardless of the specific content of a phonics program — or even in the absence of a formally outlined program — teachers should keep the following suggestions in mind.

1. *Provide a great deal of practice in auditory perception.* The groundwork is laid at the sight-word stage, when students learn to recognize similarities and differences in beginning, middle and ending sounds. Auditory perception must be developed before sound-symbol relationships can be meaningful. Dialects and generally careless pronunciation will compound the problem and increase the need for prolonged attention in this area.

2. *Proceed from the whole word to its parts.* Again, sight words will be useful. Experience shows that there is less confusion when progression is from the whole word to its parts than when letter sounds are studied first. For example, sounding can be introduced through consonant substitution: *boat* becomes *coat* when *c* is substituted for *b*.

3. *Be sure that sounding is smooth and continuous.* Inaccurate, careless pronunciation and the addition of extraneous sounds to consonants frequently cause difficulties in the application of sounding skills. The addition of an *uh* sound to consonants can be confusing: the sound of *b* is not *buh*. If the time interval between letters is kept to a minimum when blending, the tendency to interject such extraneous sounds is decreased. The letter sounds should merge. Of course students should understand from the beginning that a minor shift in accent may be all that is needed to make a word recognizable.

In *Corrective and Remedial Teaching,* Otto and McMenemy (*1966*) listed 11 phonics principles. Although there are many exceptions to each, they can be useful and are worth teaching. Some teachers reject even these principles as having too many exceptions. Students should be made aware of the exceptions whenever a principle is taught.

1. When a double consonant has a vowel on each side, only one consonant is sounded; the other is silent: narrow; fellow. *Exception:* success.

2. There are certain common combinations of consonants in which one is silent:

gn–gnarled	ps–pseudo	wr–write
kn–know	lf–calf	rh–rhythm
pn–pneumonia	mb–climb	ft–soften

In the combination *gh,* both letters are silent in many words: bough; through. *Exceptions:* tough; laugh.

3. Some consonants represent more than one sound:

> *c* like *s* if followed by *i* or *e* — circus; cent.
> *c* like *k* otherwise — cut; cat; cot.
> *g* like *j* if followed by *i* or *e* (usually) — general; ginger. *Exceptions:* get; gift.

4. The same sound is sometimes indicated by different letters or letter combinations: *j*ust; *g*esture; fu*dg*e; exa*gg*erate; gra*d*uate.

5. A final *e* is *usually* silent; it *usually* makes the preceding vowel long: rate; home; bite; cure. *Exceptions* to the long vowel: come; love; give; done.

6. Vowel combinations are *usually* pronounced with the long sound of the first vowel and the second vowel silent ("when two vowels go walking the first does the talking"): raid; team; coat; suit. *Exceptions:* aisle; buy.

7. A single vowel with a single consonant on each side, in a word or syllable, is *usually* short: pan; ten; lot; bit; bug.

8. A vowel that comes at the end of a syllable or word is usually long: pl*i* able; c*o* hort; B*i* ble.

9. A single vowel followed by *r* is pronounced as part of a glide ("*r*–controlled"): chart; dirt; hurt; pert; port.

10. A single vowel in a word or syllable, followed by *l* or *w* has a unique sound, neither short nor long: saw; ball; total.

11. Unaccented vowels are similar in sound and are indicated in many dictionaries by a schwa (upside down *e*): capit*a*l; oft*e*n; mult*i*ply; hum*o*r; murm*u*r.

Whenever phonics principles and skills are applied, students should be cautioned against being overanalytical in their approach to the reading task. Careful sounding should be reserved for truly troublesome words. Habitual overanalysis leads to slow, halting reading and interferes with efficient comprehension.

• *Structural analysis.* Instruction in structural analysis is usually divided into four areas: syllabications, inflected forms, derived forms, and compound words. Used in conjunction with phonics, structural analysis can be useful in providing clues to word meaning as well as to pronunciation.

Syllabication provides clues to pronunciation. Because syllables are pronounceable units, the tendency to interject extraneous vowel sounds common in single letter sounding is avoided. The principles of syllabication are probably best taught opportunistically as appropriate situations arise. Lists of principles vary, but the following have proved useful.

1. Each syllable has a single vowel sound.

2. A single vowel may form a syllable: *a–go; com–e–dy.*

3. A single consonant between vowels usually goes with the second vowel: *be–gan.* (There are many exceptions.)

4. When there are two consonants between vowels, the syllable division usually comes between the two consonants: *car–pet; dis–pute; fun–ny.*

5. In division of syllables, the consonant blends are kept together: *re–ply; ab–stain; con–struct.*

6. In division of syllables, prefixes and suffixes are usually separated from the root: *re–duce; will–ing–ly.*

7. In words ending in *le* preceded by a consonant, the consonant goes with the *le* in syllabication: *ta–ble.*

8. In words ending in *tion* or *sion,* the accented syllable is usually next to the last: *at–ten'–tion; con–sid–er–a'–tion.*

9. When *ed* is added to a word it forms another syllable

only when the vowel is sounded: no added syllable in *dreamed;* an added syllable in *cart–ed.*

Compound words are formed by combining two or more complete words to form a new word. The combined form usually retains the meanings of the individual words it comprises, for example, *snowshoe, smokehouse.* However, students should be cautioned about looking arbitrarily for short words in longer words. The song title, "The Last Word in Lonesome is Me," expresses a tender sentiment, but it also demonstrates the fact that finding short words in long ones leads to confusion as far as both meaning and pronunciation are concerned.

Although English is not a highly inflected language, knowledge of *inflected forms* of words can be useful both as a guide to meaning in reading and as an aid in spelling. The following generalizations regarding inflected forms may be useful. They should never be taught in isolation, but discussed in context they will lead to greater awareness of the function of root words and endings and the implications for meaning and for correct pronunciation and spelling.

1. Many root words are used exactly as they are as the base for inflectional endings:

> *ball, balls*   *talk, talking*   *sail, sailed*

2. Plurals of many words are formed by adding *s:*

> boy, boy*s*   chair, chairs

3. Plurals of words ending in *y* preceded by a consonant are formed by changing the *y* to *i* and adding *es:*

> baby, bab*ies*   pony, pon*ies*

The same plan is followed for inflectional endings other than plurals:

> (verb) carry, carri*es*   (adjective) happy, happ*ier*

4. Plurals that require an additional syllable (as following *s, x, ch,* or *sh*) are formed by adding *es:*

church, church*es*   box, box*es*   mass, mass*es*

Other inflectional endings besides plurals follow the same plan:

(verbs) catch, catch*es*   bless, bless*es*   wash, wash*es*

5. The inflectional ending for some words ending in *o* is *s,* for some *es* and for some either *s* or *es:*

radio, radio*s*   potato, potato*es*   cargo, cargo*s,* or cargo*es*

6. Words that end in final *e* drop the *e* before adding *ing, ed,* or other inflectional endings that start with a vowel:

come, com*ing*   give, giv*ing*

Exception: words ending in *ce* or *ge* retain the *e* if followed by an inflectional ending that starts with *a* or *o:* serv*iceable;* courag*eous.*

7. Words that end in final *e* usually keep the *e* before inflectional endings that start with a consonant:

mere, mer*ely*   sane, san*ely*

Exceptions: true, tru*ly;* whole, whol*ly.*

8. Many words ending in *f* form the plural by changing *f* to *v:*

wife, wi*ves*   loaf, loa*ves*

9. A syllable or a one-syllable root or base word that ends in a single consonant following a single vowel doubles the consonant before adding the inflectional ending:

tan, tan*ned*   pet, pe*tting*   sit, si*tting*   hot, ho*tter*

10. When the root word is more than one syllable, the rule above applies only if the accent is on the last syllable:

occur, occur*red*   prefer, prefer*red*

When the accent is not on the final syllable, the final consonant is usually not doubled: benefit; benefited.

11. Possession is indicated by inflectional endings as follows:

To singular nouns add *'s: the child's hat.*

To singular nouns ending in *s* add only *'* if the addition of an extra syllable is awkward: *Tom Jones's dog* or *Tom Jones' dog.*

To plural nouns not ending in *s* add *'s: the children's ball.*
To plurals ending in *s* add *'* only: *the boys' contest.*

Note: Personal pronouns have an inflectional form to indicate possession and therefore do not add an apostrophe: *its* price; *his* hair; *her* bag; the bag is *hers* or *his.*

Derived forms of words comprise word bases (roots) and prefixes or suffixes. Recognition of a familiar root word may help a reader to discover meaning, but he must understand that combination with a prefix or suffix may result in a distinct new meaning: happy, unhappy; hope, hopeless. Typically the study of prefixes, suffixes and roots is reserved for the upper grades, but newly literate adults may profit from such study at a relatively earlier stage of skill development because of their greater ability to cope with the content. Some of the more common prefixes, roots and suffixes and their meanings are listed below. Again, there are many exceptions, particularly for the suffixes. Perhaps the greatest positive effect of such study is increased interest in word origins and derivations. A sensitive teacher will know when — and if — his students are ready for this relatively sophisticated aspect of reading instruction.

· **The independent reader.** The end product of instruction in word analysis should be a repertory of skills for attacking unknown words for both pronunciation and meaning. Confronted with an unknown word, the independent reader must be able to choose from his repertory the particular attack that seems most appropriate, and, if that attack is unsuccessful, he must be able and willing to try another. A. J. Harris (*1961*, pp. 126–127) has listed a number of attacks, each of which employs one or more of the several word-analysis skills. The following list is based on Harris'.

Common Prefixes

Form	Meaning	Example
ab	off, from, away	absent, abbreviate
ad	to, toward	adventure
co, con, com, col, cor	together with	convenient, command, collect, correct
de	away, down, out of	degrade, depart
dis	not, opposite	disappear
ex	out of, formerly	export, ex-governor
in, im, il, ir	in, not	immediate, insist
pre	before	prejudice
pro	forward	progress
re	back, again	regret
un	not, opposite	unfortunate

Common Roots

duc, duct	to lead	reduce
fac, fec, fic fect, fy	to make, do	factory
mit, miss	to send	permit, remiss
pend	to hand	depend
pos, pon	to put	deposit
aspec(t)	to look	spectator
ven(t)	to go, come	advent
vert, vers	to turn	revert, adverse
scrib, script	to write	scribble, describe scripture
dic, dict	to speak	dictation

Common Suffixes

able	capable of, worth	notable
ance, ence	act or fact of doing	obedience, compliance
ancy, ency	state, quality, condition	competency
er, or	person or thing connected with, agent	teacher, director
ful	full of, abounding in	beautiful
less	without, free from	boundless
ly	like, characteristic	eagerly
ment	of state or quality	judgment
tion, sion, xion	action, state, result	relaxation

1. *Guess from context.* Indiscriminate guessing is foolish; but if a single unknown word appears in a context of known words, a considered guess is appropriate. EXAMPLE: Clyde took my picture with his new ——————— .

2. *Make use of context plus the first letter or two and the configuration of the word.* EXAMPLE: Early the next morning, Oliver went to the e——————— office. The initial *e* shows the word is probably employment rather than *doctor's* or *welfare.*

3. *Try consonant substitution.* This is appropriate when the unknown word is similar to a known word except for one or two letters, the sounds of which are known. EXAMPLE: substituting *b* for *f* makes *bought* out of *fought.* Unfortunately, though, substituting *t* for *b* does not lead from *bough* to *tough;* here context is important as a test.

4. *Divide the word into large, known parts.* EXAMPLES: post/master, super/im/position.

5. *Note that the word comprises a familiar root and an ending.* EXAMPLES: fight/ing, walk/ed, pass/es.

6. *Analyze words into known prefixes, roots, suffixes and endings.* EXAMPLES: in/depend/ence, sub/marine, beauti/ful, ex/port.

7. *Apply a phonic rule.* EXAMPLE: Application of the "first vowel long, second vowel silent" rule results in correct pronunciation of words like *boat, beat, paid* and *fruit.* But the same rule is not helpful with words like *faint, boil* and *aisle;* again, context must provide the test.

8. *Use syllabication to divide the word structurally and then sound the syllables phonically.* EXAMPLES: un/for/tu/nate, per/mit/ting.

9. *Think of an appropriate "word family."* EXAMPLE: *quill* belongs to the same "family" as *bill, fill* and *hill.*

10. *Sound the word by groups of letters and blend the sounds.* EXAMPLES: treaty = *tr-eat-y* or *tr-ea-ty* or *trea-ty;* flavor = *f-la-vor* or *fl-a-vor* or *fla-vor.*

11. *Sound the word letter by letter and blend the sounds.* EXAMPLES: print = p-r-i-n-t, plant = p-l-a-n-t.

12. *Look up the word in the dictionary.* When all else fails, or when there is a question regarding correct pronunciation or meaning the dictionary is the arbiter.

Independence in reading is not automatic once word-analysis skills have been mastered. The independent reader must have general mastery of the mechanics, but he must also comprehend what he reads. One reason for beginning with sight words is that such a procedure permits the student to deal almost immediately with meaningful thought units. Thus a basic psychological set is established at once: to read is to seek meaning.

Adults need to read. They are surrounded by written symbols that convey information. They are likely to be well aware of this fact, so the task of building a habit of constantly seeking meaning in reading will not be so great as it is with children. Nevertheless, the teacher's task is to guide and help to develop thoughtful reading from the very beginning. Awareness of context clues, interpretation of multiple meanings and figures of speech, sensitivity to objective and biased reporting, ability to grasp both stated and unstated main ideas, appreciation of relationships and implications: all these must be taught from the very beginning. Probably the best vehicles for accomplishing the task are group discussions of pertinent points as they come up in regular class work, written exercises that demand restatement of main ideas in students' own words, and exercises in which directions must be followed. Many situations in which comprehension skills can be built and stressed will arise naturally, and a good teacher will take advantage of them. Exercises to reinforce certain skills can be found in the supplementary skill builders listed in Chapter 4.

For a comprehensive curriculum guide and many specific suggestions relevant to the teaching of reading, the reader should consult the *Guide for Adult Basic Curriculum, Beginning Level,* a publication of the Bureau of Adult and Vocational Education of the U.S. Office of Education.

• FUNDAMENTALS OF TESTING

To do an effective job of teaching basic reading it is necessary to assess strengths and weaknesses of individual pupils, locate materials that meet specific instructional needs, provide instruction designed to take advantage of strengths and overcome weaknesses, examine the success in producing desired outcomes, and revise the instructional program to reflect the new findings. The process must be continuous and it must proceed from careful, frequent testing. Furthermore, adults come to basic instruction with diverse backgrounds and competencies. Some have never been taught, many have failed to learn despite prolonged teaching, others have learned but forgotten through disuse. All are unique. The function of testing is to examine the uniqueness.

In a general adult basic education program, preliminary testing is necessary to assign pupils to appropriate groups (for example, in a typical program instruction might be provided at the grade 1–3 level, the 4–6 level, and the 7–8 level). Adults who come for basic reading would, therefore, probably have already had a screening test or interview. Of course, this rough screening serves only to categorize students by broad curricular levels. Wide differences will still exist within groups. Some standardized tests that are being used for preliminary screening are: the *Gates Reading Survey* (Psychological Corporation), the *McCall-Crabbs Standard Test Lessons in Reading* (Columbia University), and the reading sections of the *Stanford* (Psychological Corporation), *Iowa* (Houghton

Mifflin Company), *SRA* (Science Research Associates), *California* (California Test Bureau) and *Metropolitan* (Harcourt, Brace and World) achievement batteries. All of these tests were written for children. With marginal literates the screening is probably best done primarily through interview, with a minimum of testing.

Opinions differ on whether a test of intellectual capacity is a necessary or even worthwhile prerequisite to basic instruction. Certainly marginally literate adults are likely to be heavily penalized by most tests. Many teachers feel that their pupils' capacity levels become obvious as instruction progresses and that there is no need for formal measures that are of questionable validity. Others feel that if they are interpreted with care, IQ scores can be useful.

If an intelligence test is to be used with marginal literates, it must have certain characteristics: (1) it must not have items that require reading ability; (2) it should have as little class or cultural bias as possible; (3) administration time should be reasonably short, particularly if the test must be administered individually; and (4) the format should not be juvenile. Some non-verbal tests are available, and they do offer the advantage of requiring no reading. But they have limited value when the purpose for testing is to get prognostic information regarding achievement. Reading is a verbal skill; therefore, it is highly related to other verbal abilities. Picture vocabulary tests are highly verbal in content and they meet the other criteria fairly well. The *Full Range Picture Vocabulary Test* and the *Quick Test* (Psychological Test Specialists) yield estimates of verbal intelligence based on hearing vocabulary. In testing, the examiner enunciates a word and the subject chooses a picture that matches the meaning of the word. The subject need not read, write or speak to respond. The *Peabody Picture Vocabulary Test* (American Guidance Service) is similar, but the norms range from age 2 through 18 only. Each can be given in 3 to 15 minutes and scored quickly. Group tests that require no reading are also available, but they are designed for use in the primary grades and they tend to be less verbally oriented.

After screening tests have been given, the task is to determine specific strengths and weaknesses of individual pupils. In a typical basic reading group, some pupils will be almost completely unable to read even single words, others will have fairly extensive sight vocabularies, and still others have some word recognition skills. In order to make use of existing skills, locate suitable materials, and determine the appropriate starting place in a program of instruction, the teacher will need to do further testing. Of course, the need for constant re-testing remains even when instruction is underway. A few of the systems described in Chapter 4 include their own placement tests, but most do not. The discussion that follows includes suggestions for testing adults. Again the task is complicated by the fact that many of the basic tests were devised for children, but useful tests are available.

Informal Reading Inventories

The informal inventory was first described by Betts (*1957*, Ch. 21), and is now widely accepted as a means for observing pupils' oral and silent reading at different difficulty levels. Informal inventories offer these advantages: they comprise material commonly used in the classroom, so that they are readily available and inexpensive; derived estimates of ability are likely to be valid because actual teaching materials are used; they can be used to sample a wide range of skills and competencies. Checklists can be used in conjunction with the inventories to systematize observations of various skills.

An inventory can easily be constructed. Elementary school teachers use graded series of readers, but literacy instructors will do better to choose adult materials at progressive difficulty levels. First, the teacher chooses four or five books, ranging from the very beginning level to one of approximately fourth-grade difficulty. Then he chooses selections from well within each book. Selection length may vary from four or five sentences at the easiest level to about 100 words at the most difficult level. Finally, he prepares four questions that require thoughtful answers for each selection. Once prepared, the inventory can be used repeatedly.

To administer the test the teacher simply has the student read the progressively more difficult selections and answer the questions for each. The student may be asked to read silently or orally, depending on the information sought. Oral reading provides clues about sight vocabulary, word attack skills and phrasing, but comprehension tests are more valid after silent reading. Four levels of reading ability can be established:

1. *Independent level.* There should be not more than one error in word recognition and three out of four correct answers to comprehension questions. This is the level at which the student can read on his own. Books for recreational reading can be on this level.

2. *Instructional level.* There may be up to five word-recognition errors in a 100-word selection, but comprehension should remain at least 75 percent. Proper names and repeated prompts should not be counted as word-recognition errors. This is the level at which the student can read with limited teacher supervision, and it is probably the appropriate level for instructional materials.

3. *Frustration level.* This is the level at which word-recognition accuracy is less than 95 percent and/or comprehension is less than 50 percent. Materials at this level include too many words that are unfamiliar or undecipherable with existing word-analysis skills and/or too complex sentences or concepts to permit even minimal comprehension.

4. *Hearing capacity level.* At this level the student can answer three out of four questions based on materials read to him. Determination of this level provides the teacher with some notion of the level of material the student could handle if he had the necessary word-analysis skills. For the

adult who is just learning to read this is probably not a good indication of ultimate capacity; the level is likely to go up as his general verbal abilities increase.

The informal inventory can be one of the literacy instructor's most useful tools. It can be used to determine initial placement, to group students for instruction, and to evaluate progress throughout the instructional sequence. Aside from its use as a measuring instrument, the informal inventory offers still another advantage. Everyone agrees that an adult can be frightened away from a basic education program by testing. The informal inventory in the hands of a sensitive teacher has none of the formidability of standardized tests. A possible disadvantage is that it must be administered individually, but the time involved is not great and the results are available at once.

Smith and Smith (*1962*) have suggested a check sheet that may be helpful when an inventory is given to each adult in a group. The check sheet that follows is an adaptation. Other revisions may be needed in other situations. One example of a ready-made informal inventory is Smith's *Graded Selections for Informal Diagnosis*. It may be useful as a guide to the preparation of an original inventory, but its child-oriented content and format make it inappropriate for direct use with adults. Another commercially prepared inventory is *The Adult Basic Reading Inventory* (Scholastic Testing Service), which also includes tests of sight-word recognition and sound and letter discrimination.

Other Informal Techniques

Teachers of adult basic reading make extensive use of informal testing. The tests may be as broad in scope as the informal inventory or as specific as a brief test designed to check knowledge of the alphabet. They can be tailored to the specific needs of an instructional program and of individual students, they can be used at any time, and the results are immediately available. But the fact that the tests are informal

INFORMAL INVENTORY CHECK SHEET

NAME _____ DATE _____

Word Recognition

Sounds added	____	Phonics clues not used	____
Sounds omitted	____	Context clues not used	____
Words confused	____	Syllabication not used	____
Reversals	____	Vowel sounds confused	____
Endings omitted	____	_____	
Mispronunciations	____	_____	
Letter transposed	____	_____	

Examples of errors: _____

_____

_____

Comprehension

Word-by-word reading	____
Lack of phrasing	____
Frequent repetitions	____
Missed detail questions	____
Missed main idea questions	____

Other Difficulties

_____

_____

_____

Reading Levels

Books used _____

Independent	_____
Instructional	_____
Frustration	_____
Capacity	_____

Materials recommended _____

_____

should not imply that they can be casually thrown together. Informal tests must be carefully prepared, for if they are to be useful they must be interesting, at the proper difficulty level, and aimed at a specific objective.

· **A check for readability.** One of the things that teachers need to check constantly is whether a particular book can be read by a particular student at a particular time. That a book is rated at a certain "grade level" of difficulty provides little specific help; too many factors combine to make a book readable or not readable for a specific adult. Likewise, although readability formulas are available for rating books, they are unwieldly to use and they yield scores with all the limitations of a publisher's grade level rating. Two plans for quick, informal readability checks are, therefore, suggested. First, a variation of the informal inventory may be useful. Available books may each have a standard-length passage designated on a certain page — say about 100 words on page 20 — and a set of questions based on the passage glued inside the back cover. To determine whether a student is able to read a certain book, he is merely asked to read the selection and answer the questions. Thus, whether the book is at his independent, instructional or frustration level is very simply determined. Second, a quick check of ability to cope with the vocabulary in a book can be obtained by listing a sample of words — say the third word on every fifth page — on a sheet glued inside the back cover. If the student knows all the words, chances are he can read the book.

· **Word lists.** Well selected word lists can be used for several diagnostic purposes. Inability to respond quickly when the words are presented suggests a limited sight vocabulary and implies lack of fluency in reading. Attempts to analyze words not known at sight reveal strengths and weaknesses in word attack. Inability to cope with a basic word list suggests that the student will have difficulty in reading materials developed from that list. Some of the better instructional materials for adults include lists of words used at the back of each book,

This practice is to be encouraged, for it provides the teacher with a useful tool.

• **Evaluation of specific skills and abilities.** Very brief, informal tests can be devised to provide answers to specific questions. Formal tests, for example, often get at word discrimination (picking the correct word from among several) rather than word analysis (attacking words in isolation) skills. With an informal test, a teacher can quickly check both word-discrimination and word-analysis skills. Likewise, the teacher can use informal tests to check ability to apply phonic principles, syllabication generalizations and blending skills; to compare oral and silent reading rate; to ascertain level of comprehension; and many other abilities. Informal tests may be patterned after items or subtests from standardized tests. Some instructional systems include frequent, brief informal tests for use at the teacher's discretion. Kottmeyer (*1965*9), pp. 91–97) has suggested a number of common questions and exercises that are useful for informal diagnosis.

Standarized Tests

In addition to the survey type reading tests discussed earlier, a number of diagnostic tests are available. Many of them are appropriate for use with adults despite the fact that they were intended for children; the contents and formats are not generally childish. Care should be taken to prepare adult pupils for standardized tests; they are likely to feel threatened and uncomfortable in the testing situation. Nevertheless, there is value in helping adults to achieve some degree of test sophistication because they are likely to be tested for other purposes outside the classroom. If students understand that tests are measures of progress rather than final arbiters of success, they will usually come to accept them without overanxiety.

A few examples of both group and individually administered diagnostic tests are given here. The list is intended to be merely illustrative, not exhaustive.

• **Group tests.** Tests that can be administered to groups offer the obvious advantage of economy of administration time. If student responses are carefully analyzed, group tests can yield useful information.

The Bond-Clymer-Hoyt *Silent Reading Diagnostic Tests* (Lyons and Carnahan) comprise 11 subtests bound in a single test booklet. The following subtests are included: (1) *Word Recognition;* (2) *Recognition of Words in Context;* (3) *Recognition of Reversible Words in Context;* (4) *Word-Recognition Techniques: Visual Analysis-Locating Usable Elements;* (5) *Word-Recognition Techniques: Visual Analysis-Syllabication;* (6) *Word-Recognition Techniques: Visual Analysis-Locating Root Words;* (7) *Phonetic Knowledge-General Word Element;* (8) *Recognition of Beginning Sounds;* (9) *Rhyming Sounds;* (10) *Letter Sounds;* (11) *Word Synthesis.* Administration of the test is uncomplicated, as is the scoring. Two types of scores can be derived from the subtests: scores in word recognition (sight recognition) and scores in word-analysis techniques. The tests are intended for use in grades three through six, but there is nothing to make them offensive to an adult. They will be most useful after the student has gotten well into Stage Two of basic reading instruction.

The *Doren Diagnostic Reading Test* (Education Test Bureau) is a measure of word recognition skill mastery. Subtests sample skills in the following areas: letter recognition (manuscript and cursive), beginning sounds, whole-word recognition, words within words, speech consonants, ending sounds, blending, rhyming, vowels, sight words and discriminate guessing (use of context clues). The test can be used whenever a thorough analysis of word attack skills is desired. It is easy to give and to score.

Other group tests that may be useful are the diagnostic subtests of the *Diagnostic Reading Tests* (Committee on Diagnostic Reading Tests) and Test A (vocabulary) and B (paragraph comprehension) of the *Iowa Every-Pupil Test of Basic Skills* (Houghton Mifflin).

· **Individual tests.** One obvious advantage of individual

testing is that it permits observation of oral reading per-
formanance, and the most straightforward way to assess phrasing and many word-analysis difficulties is through oral reading.
By observing oral reading performance, a teacher can determine whether a student has an adequate sight vocabulary,
whether he has a method for attacking unknown words, and
whether he uses context clues. The teacher can also note
faulty reading habits such as word substitutions, omissions
of letters and words, lack of phrasing, disregard for punctuation and repetition of words and phrases.

A good example of a standardized oral reading test is the
Gilmore Oral Reading Test (Harcourt, Brace and World).
The test comprises 10 paragraphs of increasing difficulty,
ranging from about first- to tenth-grade level. The paragraphs
are on heavy cardboard, spiral bound into a booklet that presents a continuous story. Separate record booklets are available. The manual includes a code for recording several types
of errors: substitutions, mispronunciations, words pronounced
by the examiner, disregard of punctuation, insertions, hesita-
tions, omissions and repetitions. There are grade-level norms
for accuracy, comprehension and rate. Two forms are available. The test can serve as a model for teachers who wish to
devise informal oral tests of their own. Similar tests of oral
reading are the *Gray Oral Reading Test* (Bobbs-Merrill) and
the older *Gray Standardized Oral Reading Check Tests*
(Bobbs-Merrill).

Another advantage of individual testing is that it permits
the teacher to probe for detailed and extensive information
regarding reading skill development on a highly personalized
basis. Any one of the three standardized tests for individual
diagnosis discussed here will be useful for detailed analysis
of reading skills. Administration is time consuming, but
efficiency can be gained by using only those subtests that are
most pertinent. Teachers who intend to use the tests must be
thoroughly familiar with administration and scoring procedures before reliable and valid sampling can be expected.

The *Durrell Analysis of Reading Difficulty* (Harcourt, Brace and World), the *Gates-McKillop Reading Diagnostic Tests* (Columbia University), and the *Diagnostic Reading Scales* by George Spache (California Test Bureau) are individual tests for reading diagnosis. They are similar in that each includes an oral reading test and a variety of other subtests designed to sample widely from the skill areas essential to basic reading achievement. While each is probably satisfactory for use with adults at the basic level, we prefer the *Gates-McKillop,* which is described in detail by way of example.

The complete kit of the *Gates-Mc*Killop Reading Diagnostic *Tests* includes two equivalent forms of the entire battery, spiral-bound testing material, pupil record blanks, an examiner's manual and tachistoscopic cards. The following subtests make up the diagnostic battery:

1. *Oral Reading.* The test comprises seven paragraphs of increasing difficuly, ranging from second- to eighth-grade level.

2. *Words: Flash Presentation.* Two columns of progressively more difficult words are given. A hand tachistoscope is used to expose each word for about one-half second. Incorrect responses are recorded, to be examined later for error types.

3. *Words: Untimed Presentation.* The format is similar to the flash presentation test, but the pupil is encouraged to take all the time he needs to figure out each word.

4. *Phrases: Flash Presenation.* The format and procedure is similar to the flash presentation of words test, but 26 phrases of progressively greater length and difficulty are given.

5. *Knowledge of Word Parts: Word Attack.* Four subtests are included. (a) *Recognition and Blending Common Word Parts: Nonsense Words* (e.g., *drite, frable, brome*) are used to test ability to blend common word parts into wholes.

(b) *Giving Letter Sounds:* The student is asked to give the sound for single lower case letters. (c, d) *Naming Capital Letters: Naming Lower Case Letters:* This basic test to determine knowledge of the alphabet is used only when appropriate.

6. *Recognizing the Visual Form of Sounds.* Four subtests are employed to assess ability to associate sounds with their visual (word or letter) equivalents. (a) *Nonsense Words:* The examiner enunciates a nonsense word (e.g., *tabe*) and the student picks its visual equivalent from a group of four nonsense words (e.g., *tode, tabe, kib, bate*). (b) *Initial Letters:* The examiner enunciates a word and the student picks its initial letter from a list of five letters. (c) *Final Letters:* The student picks the final letter of a word enunciated by the examiner from a list of five letters. (d) *Vowels:* The examiner enunciates a nonsense word with a vowel sound in the middle (e.g., *keb, kine*) and the student identifies the vowel that "makes the sound."

7. *Auditory Blending.* The examiner enunciates a total of 15 words part by part, and the student "tells what each word is" (e.g., *f-ire-cra-ker:* firecracker).

8. *Supplementary Tests.* The four supplementary tests may be used when certain information is lacking or when the other subtests reveal that further checking is needed. (a) *Spelling:* The student is asked to spell the 40 words from the flash presentation list orally. The examiner observes the attack used (e.g., phonetic spelling, letter-by-letter, common errors, etc.). (b) *Oral Vocabulary:* According to the Manual, this test may be used in the absence of the *Stanford Binet* oral vocabulary test. With adults, the test may have prognostic value similar to the picture vocabulary tests. (c) *Syllabication:* The student divides nonsense words into syllables. The test measures ability to recognize syllables outside the context of meaningful words. (d) *Auditory Discrimination:* The examiner enunciates a pair

of words (*do–to*) and the student is asked whether they are the same or different.

The subtests of the *Gates-McKillop* sample from a wide range of skills and from different skill-development levels. A teacher will profit from becoming familiar with the subtests even though he may never use the entire test at one sitting. Perhaps the most efficient practice with adults is to use individual subtests as needed to get specific information. The subtests can also serve as models for the teacher as he makes his own informal tests. For this reason, it is worthwhile to be familiar with all three of the test batteries discussed. In practice, a good plan is to be able to administer one of the three effectively and to be familiar with the general content of the other two.

Intensive Diagnosis

Most adult students will respond satisfactorily to instruction that is carefully planned on the basis of specific testing. Some will need extra help from time to time in order to get over rough spots, but informal testing will generally help the teacher to identify and meet these needs as they arise. However, it is realistic to expect a few students to have some severe learning problems. Such cases are common among children who are learning to read, and there is every reason to believe that among adults in basic reading the incidence will be even greater. Through natural selection, a group of marginally literate adults is apt to include a number of severe learning problem cases.

No attempt is made here to deal with the diagnosis and treatment of severe learning problems. These topics demand coverage that is beyond the scope of this book. The reader is referred to Otto and McMenemy's *Corrective and Remedial Teaching* for an approach that may be useful in tackling such problems. To assume that an approach to children's learning problems could be adopted across the board would be naive, but many of the basic principles and techniques can be adapted.

Teachers' capacities for dealing with severe learning problems will differ, just as their proficiencies differ. Some will be able to provide a great deal of special help and do intensive diagnoses and others will not. Time limitations, too, will be an important factor. For those who have limited backgrounds in corrective and remedial teaching, the following generalizations may be helpful, at least as a basis for gaining some perspective.

1. Some adults will have great difficulty learning to read despite their average or better intelligence and their successful achievement in other areas.

2. The causes for disability in reading are diverse. Seldom can a single factor be isolated as the sole cause; instead, several factors are likely to be interacting.

3. Adequate diagnosis of severe learning problems is likely to entail intensive case-study analysis. Referral of individuals to experts in other fields — medical specialists, speech therapists, psychotherapists, audiologists, social workers, etc. — may be necessary.

4. Instruction of students with severe learning disabilities is usually most effectively done on an individual, or individualized, basis. Careful instrumental diagnosis is mandatory.

· PRINCIPLES FOR TEACHING

The discussion here is focused upon principles that will be useful in teaching beginning reading to adults. The basic reading teacher ought also to be familiar with characteristics of adult learners, with general techniques for teaching adults, and with broad principles of adult learning. Three very readable books published by the National Association of Public School Adult Educators are recommended: *How Adults Can*

Learn More — Faster; When You're Teaching Adults; and A Treasury of Techniques for Teaching Adults.

The teaching principles listed below are based upon validated learning principles. They provide the framework upon which an instructional program can be built.

• **1. Motivation must be sustained.** With children who are learning to read, lack of motivation is a common problem. With adults who have enrolled in a basic education class, it is not likely to be a major problem. However, adults' motivation may have very different bases. For example, a father may have a short-range goal of reading his son's letters or a long-range goal of acquiring the training needed for a better job. To secure maximum cooperation in the learning situation, the teacher must understand the basis for each learner's motivation. And early motivation must be sustained. Some adults will expect too much, too fast. They will need guidance in setting realistic goals. Some will have other activities competing for their time. They will need the teacher's empathy and counsel as they gain perspective. Perhaps most important, all need to make continuous short-term progress that is meaningful to them.

• **2. Instruction should make use of the learner's strength.** The teacher must know each student's level of skill development and ability to progress. Both testing and careful observation will provide the basis for this knowledge. Adults tend to be more realistic than children. They can be brought to recognize their limitations, but they will respond enthusiastically to an appeal to their strengths. The teachers must also know and have access to a wide range of materials, either commercially or opportunistically prepared, in order to exploit each learner's special skills, competencies, interests and abilities.

• **3. Effective instruction is carefully paced, sequential and productive.** While every effort should be made to make use of what the adult learned has, it is important to consider what he does not have. Typically, the sub-literate adult is overwhelmed by the mass of reading material that surrounds him. He does not have the ability to break into an instructional sequence without guidance, or the capacity to absorb instruction without repetition, or the patience to accept instruction that does not move him steadily and perceptibly toward his own goals.

The teacher's initial task is to help each student to begin at the appropriate place in an instructional program. The next task is to pursue an orderly sequence of skill development at a pace that is appropriate for the learner. To make this task manageable, the sequence of a carefully chosen instructional program should be followed, but the pace must be adapted to individual needs. Each step in the sequence should be repeated — through review, evaluation, reteaching and re-evaluation — until readiness for the next step is assured. Isolated drill has little value, but repetition to the point of mastery is invaluable.

Unlike children, adults do not comprise a captive audience. They are likely to withdraw if results are not concrete and immediate. When principles and skills are learned, they should be applied at once in meaningful reading situations. With adults, there is not so much need to worry about reinforcing success experiences with extrinsic "things" like jelly beans, gold stars or pats on the head. A perceptible step toward a personal goal carries much intrinsic reinforcement.

• **4. Learning tasks and materials should be based upon familiar experiences.** Adults bring a wide background of experiences to the learning situation, so it is not necessary to spend as much instructional time developing meanings and concepts as with children. Instead, the effective teacher will make use of existing experiences and take advantage of the insights and the ability to grasp relationships that come with maturity. Adults will learn rapidly and enthusiastically to recognize words and read materials that are tied to previous experience. They will appreciate the appeal to their existing knowledge, and the teacher will avoid the tendency to "talk down" when giving basic instruction.

• **5. Instruction should be structured to facilitate remembering.** Forgetting is due primarily to interference; that is, old learnings block new learnings and new learnings blur old learnings because similarities in what is known and what is being learned tend to merge. The teacher should take care to stress the unique features of new learning; differentiation will combat interference. On the other hand, of course, students must see relationships if they are to grasp relationships and form genealizations. Uniqueness and similarity can be stressed concurrently.

In some learning, remembering is best expedited by over-learning. For example, frequently used words ought to be recognized instantly in reading, and the best way to ensure instant recognition is to provide repetitive practice. Tachisto-scopic presentation via a projection device may help to relieve monotony, and distributed practice is more effective than massed, but the fact is that repetitive pracice is drill. Adults will accept it if they understand the need and the payoff.

• CLASSROOM MANAGEMENT

The specifics of classroom management must be evolved within a particular administrative framework, so what can be said here that would be applicable for all, or even most, classrooms is limited. Yet there are problems having to do with directing and shaping the classroom situation that are fairly common and that concern many teachers.

Whether the enrollment policy will be open or term is not within teachers' immediate control, but there are major im-plications for the classroom set-up. With *term enrollment,* all students come into the program with the understanding that the sessions will cover a predetermined number of ses-sions or weeks. The teacher can plan a developmental se-quence to cover the time available, but provision must be made for starting each student at the appropriate level and for grouping by instructional needs once the class has begun. With _open enrollment,_ students enter and leave the class as they wish. The teacher must be able to assimilate new arrivals into appropriate existing groups on the basis of their skill development. If this can be done successfully, the open set-up offers possibilities for flexibility that cannot be found in the closed. In general, the adult newcomer will be able to join a group with little difficulty because he can cope with a new situation more readily than a child can. On the other hand, the teacher's task is to pick the right group, to provide an instructional transition — which may be readiness activity for the newcomer and review for the others — and to regroup as needed. Adaptability on the part of the teacher is the key to success with open enrollment; some teachers will thrive and others will flounder. In an ideal program there might be both term and open classes. Such an arrangement would meet the needs of all pupils and give teachers the option of working in the situations they find most comfortable. Of course, if the teaching set-up is primarily tutorial the concerns are not the same.

The teacher must also adapt the classroom set-up in terms of length of class periods, frequency of class meetings and the limit, if any, of total meetings available. These considerations have implications for materials to be used and for pace and depth of instruction. Some instructional systems have a suggested time schedule for completion of the program up to a certain proficiency level. Obviously, there can be no set predetermination of pace, for individuals must be considered, but there can be general pacing in terms of depth of coverage of certain skills and supporting information and activities.

Class size is generally an administrative decision. The consensus is that up to about 15 students can be taught effectively in a class. Some rule of thumb is necessary to expedite planning, but it should be clear that while 15 may be an appropriate average class size, it is not a magic number. Enrollees in basic reading classes range from bright, highly skilled tradesmen, who for some reason were never taught to read, to slow or problem learners who never learned despite much teaching, and from aged immigrants to young mothers. They may be in class because they themselves decided to come or because they have been included in some special program. A sensible procedure is to adapt class size to the nature of the group. For example, a class might realistically include more than 15 students if they are all bright young men who are eager to make up for lost time, but individual or very small group instruction would be appropriate for students with low intelligence or severe learning problems.

Whether a class meets during the day or in the evening may have implications for instruction. Evening classes are likely to include persons who have worked all day at a regular job, so the teacher must consider the special problem of fatigue. Evening students may be particularly anxious to make rapid progress in order to see the payoff in job upgrading. With day students there may be more opportunities for field trips and other activities.

Progress records should be kept for each student. The record should be cumulative for the entire time the student spends in a program, but the basic reading teacher is likely to have responsibility for starting the record because he will see the student first. There is no need for an elaborate record, but care should be taken to include primarily objective data, to demonstrate development over a period of time, and to make the record available and useful to other professional staff members. The reading teacher ought to see that the results of preliminary and progress tests, both formal and informal, are included. Where there is provision for testing by level of competency and the awarding of certificates of competency, the record should show each successive level reached. Many teachers feel that certificates of competency — awarded at frequent intervals for the completion of identifiable development steps — provide tangible rewards for the attainment of short-term goals that are important to many marginally literate adults. Special needs and special competencies of the student should be noted as they are observed. For example, significant changes in attitude, severe physical or emotional problems, special family circumstances, outstanding aptitudes, and deviations from expected progress are the kinds of special information that ought to be included.

Related to the demonstration of competency is the need for systematic evaluation. Formal requirements will be determined by the administration, but most programs will include some means for demonstrating both the success of individuals and the success of the total program. The necessary precaution here is to prepare students for testing. Formal tests, particularly timed tests, are likely to evoke a fear response in marginally literate adults, probably because such tests are associated with early school failure or with an expectation of failure. As pointed out in the discussion on testing, adults should be prepared for tests by being shown that they are useful in shaping further learning and that they are likely to be encountered in situations outside the classroom.

A final point in regard to testing: most of the standardized tests that are commonly used for testing adults' basic reading achievement yield grade equivalency scores that are a year or more above students' functional level. Teachers need to know what to expect from each test that they use. When they do, they can make informal adjustments or do corroborative rechecks as needed to make the results most useable.

• A FINAL WORD

The teacher of adult basic reading faces a unique challenge, but this is not the place to repeat standard clichés about the art and joys of teaching. Most of the people who read this book will have heard them all. The final word is simply this: With most of your students, others have tried and failed. If you fail, there probably will be no more trying.

• REFERENCES

BETTS, E. A. *Foundations of Reading Instruction*. New York: American Book, 1957.

DOLCH, E. W. "A Basic Sight Vocabulary." *The Elementary School Journal*, 36:456–460, February, 1936.

GREEN, EDITH S. (ED.) *Guide for Adult Basic Curriculum, Beginning Level*. Washington: Bureau of Adult and Vocational Education, U.S. Department of Health, Education and Welfare, 1966.

HARRIS, A. J. *How To Increase Reading Ability*. Fourth Edition. New York: David McKay, 1961.

KOTTMEYER, W. *Teacher's Guide to Remedial Reading*. St. Louis: Webster, 1959.

OTTO, WAYNE, AND RICHARD A. MCMENEMY. *Corrective and Remedial Teaching*. Boston: Houghton Mifflin, 1966.

SMITH, E. H., AND MARIE P. SMITH. *Teaching Reading to Adults*. Washington: National Association of Public School Adult Educators, 1962.

SMITH, NILA B. *Graded Selections for Informal Reading Diagnosis, Grades 1 through 3*. New York: New York University Press, 1959.

• PUBLISHERS' ADDRESSES

American Guidance Service, 720 Washington Avenue, S.E., Minneapolis, Minnesota 55414

The Bobbs-Merrill Co., Inc., 4300 West 62nd Street, Indianapolis, Indiana 46206

California Test Bureau, 5916 Hollywood Boulevard, Los Angeles, California 90028

Columbia University, Teachers College, Bureau of Publications, 525 West 20th Street, New York, New York 10027

Committee on Diagnostic Reading Tests, Mountain Home, North Carolina 28758

Educational Test Bureau, 720 Washington Avenue, S.E., Minneapolis, Minnesota 55414

Harcourt, Brace & World, Inc., 757 Third Avenue, New York, New York 10017

Houghton Mifflin Company, 110 Tremont Street, Boston, Massachusetts 02107

Lyons & Carnahan, 407 East 25th Street, Chicago, Illinois 60616

Psychological Corporation, 304 East 45th Street, New York, New York 10017

Psychological Test Specialists, Box 1441, Missoula, Montana 59801

Science Research Associates, Inc., 259 East Erie Street, Chicago, Illinois 60611

Scholastic Testing Service, 480 Meyer Road, Bensenville, Illinois 60106

INDEX

Index does not include titles or authors of the materials listed in Chapter 4.